STALINGRAD: STRUGGLE IN THE EAST

CHRISTIAN SHAKESPEARE

Copyright © 2014 Christian Shakespeare

All rights reserved.

ISBN: 1499508174

ISBN-13: 978-1499508178

CONTENTS

PREFACE

German Attitude Toward the Soviet Union   2

Soviet Relations & the Molotov-Ribbentrop Pact   5

PART I – THE BLOODY ROAD TO STALINGRAD

Barbarossa: Germany Assaults the Soviet Union   15

1942 Summer Offensive: 33
Case Blue: Hitler's Thirst for Russian Oil

The Axis Order of Battle   38

Standing Ground – The Soviet Defenders   42

Axis Charge into Southern Russia   45

Army Group A: Operation Edelweiss: 50
Smashing into the Caucasus

The Oil Rich Regions   55

The Luftwaffe Strikes   60

Army Group B: Operation Heron: 63
The Drive East to the Volga

PART II – THE BATTLE FOR STALIN'S CITY

Stalingrad - The Beginning of the Assault   69

Inner City Murder   78

The Luftwaffe Strikes Again   92

The German Flank is Exposed…   98

The Russian Fight Back – Operation Uranus	103
The Axis Situation *is* Dangerous	110
The Red Army Masses...	116
The Red Army Strikes	122
Romanian Targets in the North	125
The German Southern Flank	130
Russian Jaws - The Closing of the Trap	133
Awful Reality – The Fate of the Sixth Army	144

PART III – CATASTROPHE!!

Operation Winter Storm	153
The Soviet Defence	159
Von Manstein to the Rescue	163
The Soviet Response	168
German Inadequacy and Collapse	172
The Legacy of a Failed Plan	178
Red Storm Turns the Tide: Operation Little Saturn	182
First Phase – December 1942	185
Second Phase – January 1943	195
Operation Koltso – Russian Victory	206

After the Guns Fall Silent	218
Casualties	232

CONCLUSION

One City Too Far	236

PREFACE

"When the attack on Russia starts the world will hold its breath…and make no comment"
(Hitler, 1941)

1

German Attitude Toward the Soviet Union

The Second World War was without a doubt the single most, bloody conflict in history. Of all the many fronts fought in many different countries none was fought with such racial hatred and ideological harshness as the Eastern Front. The roots of the struggle in the east could be traced back to 1925 in Adolf Hitler's Mein Kampf, where he openly argues for the necessity for *Lebensraum,* or living space for Germanic peoples in the East. In Mein Kampf, Hitler stresses that the African colonies under Keiser Wilhelm II's Imperial Germany (the *Keiserreich*) which were lost to the allies after World War I were of less importance. Germany, he argues must look to expansionism in the East, at the expense of

Russia.

Nazi Ideology observed Eastern Europe as being populated by Slavs, which they saw as an inferior race with the Soviet Union in particular being ruled by Jews. These 'Jewish Bolsheviks' was seen as the racial and ideological opposition to the so-called German 'Master Race'. According to Mein Kampf, the ultimate destiny of Germany was to turn east as it did six hundred years previously, rationalising this policy by pompously declaring that the end of Jewish domination in Russia will be the end of Russia as a state. The "Pan-Slav ideals" was to be the basis for which an eventual confrontation could not be avoided for which the prize would be, Hitler argued, "permanent mastery of the world."

Due to the political differences, Nazi Germany, the right wing nationalist one-party state and the Soviet Union, the left-wing federal socialist state was completely opposed to one another. Basically the Nazi policy toward the Soviet Union was one where it was acceptable to kill, deport or at the very least, enslave the Russian and Slavic peoples under the umbrella of a racial doctrine; a doctrine which justified the physical, physiological and intellectual humiliation of anyone the Nazis considered inferior to their own ideals.

2

Soviet Relations & the Molotov-Ribbentrop Pact

The situation in the Soviet Union though was very different. Not wishing to antagonise Hitler, the first inclinations of movement in the east came publically in August 1939, right on the verge of war. Hitler, who expressed concern at moves in London to negotiate a pact with Moscow, which had been going on since March of that year, decided to strike first; but not militarily, but diplomatically. Negotiations between the British and the Russians had been lacklustre at best since the Russians feared western capitalism and wanted nothing more than a solid military alliance with both the British and the French. However, after Stalin's

Great Officer Purge, both the allies believed that the Soviet Union could not be a main and strong enough participant in curbing Germany's increasingly belligerent foreign stance. This uncertainty and instability between the West and the East played directly into an advantage for the Nazis. While the USSR was talking to the West, both Russian and German representatives began issuing statements regarding the feasibility of political negotiations between April and June. Any potential deal at the time had to set out a measure of common ground; an economic framework for which the two nations could base talks on. This was largely because any other links such as military ties had been completely severed since the middle of the 1930's. In May, Stalin appointed Vyacheslav Molotov as his foreign minister to replace the Jewish and pro-western Maxim Litvinov and this allowed the USSR to become more appealing to a wider sphere of influence such as Germany. Negotiations between Russian and German parties continued into July of 1939 where most of the economic details had been worked out by early August which allowed for further talks into a political agreement. By the beginning of August both countries had worked out the economic aspects of a deal and talks had now advanced enough to put forward the idea of a political alliance. The basis for this was that both Soviet Russia and Nazi Germany had similar aggressive foreign policies, citing anti-capitalism as a justification for doing so. Meanwhile at the same time, Russian negotiations were scheduled to continue with both Britain and France in Moscow on military matters in the same month. The aim of this three party talk was to discuss what the reaction would be between these nations in the event of a German attack. However the talks stalled somewhat on a technical issue, the granting of military passage of Soviet troops through Poland if Germany was to assault the east. Russia wanted both Britain and France to pressurise the Polish to agree to Russian demands but Poland refused to allow the Soviet Red Army on its territory should Germany attack. Throughout August 1939 this seemed to be Hitler's next logical target after his invasion of Czechoslovakia and the Czech-Slovak partition back in March. The Poles justified this stubbornness by pointing out that if they allowed the Russian armies to occupy their territory, they feared they would never leave given that the majority of Polish territory, particularly the eastern territories were carved out of the old Imperial Russia and the west from the old Prussian lands of the former German Empire at the end of the First World War.

Their independence was recognised by the Treaty of Versailles and the military history between the Poland and Russia was aggressive; between 1919 and 1921, both countries engaged in an armed conflict called the Polish-Soviet War which ended in victory for Poland signed by the Treaty of Riga. This history fuelled the Polish attitude toward the USSR and the west and therefore provided a major sticking point in the Russo-Allied tripartite military talks. Meanwhile on the 19 August, economic negotiations continued between Moscow and Berlin, finally resulting in the 1939 German-Soviet Commercial Agreement. This meant that the USSR would receive credit from Germany at a level of 200 million Reichsmarks over a seven year period set at an interest rate of 4.5 percent.

The agreement was that with this credit, Russia could buy capital goods such as transport vehicles and factory equipment with a view to paying Germany off by material shipment back into the Reich (goods and equipment) from 1946 onwards. This arrangement prompted the Soviet Union to break down its tripartite talks with both Britain and France on the 21 August on which Stalin himself received assurances that Germany would approve a secret protocol embedded in a proposed non-aggression pact between the two nations.

The next day, the 22 August, Moscow announced Stalin would receive the German foreign minister Joachim von Ribbentrop within 24 hours. Yet the Russians were still even at this stage, negotiating with both the British and French diplomats in the capital, but it was nothing short of a stalemate as the western powers were not willing to concede to the Soviets certain aspects of any such deal. Blocked in his talks with the allies, Stalin instead turned to Germany with whom he had now improving economic and military relations, and entered into the secret Nazi-Soviet pact. By the 24 August a non-aggression pact was signed for 10 years with a condition that either nation would remain neutral if one or the other went to war with another country. This was more suited to Hitler who, fearing an alliance of nations from both directions, and knowing that the main threat came from the western powers, now had his eastern borders protected if Germany pushed the world to war. To ensure the successful conclusion of the deal, Ribbentrop was given a sweetener; the secret protocol in the proposed non-aggression pact included a dividing up of nations into what was called 'spheres of influence'. In the north, Finland, Estonia and Latvia were assigned to the Soviet sphere while Lithuania would come under German influence. But it was Poland where the greatest partition was drawn up. Clearly Germany planned to invade Poland and Stalin was promised the whole of the eastern side of the country directly absorbed into the Soviet Union; territory running east of the San, Narev, Vistula and Pisa rivers. Anything west of these would come under German occupation including Warsaw. Other clauses of the protocol granted the city of Vilnius to Lithuania away from Polish control and the promise that Germany would not interfere in the USSR's actions toward eastern Romania, the territory of Bessarabia. As a result, this region was eventually to be joined to Moldova and come under direct control of Moscow as the Moldovan SSR. By the 24 August 1939 the Nazi-Soviet Pact was announced (minus the secret protocol) to a stunned world. Two ideological enemies had found common ground enough to sign a non-aggression pact, and were immediately confirmed with pictures from the Russian capital showing the signing and meeting between Ribbentrop and Stalin himself. It was a surprise since the relations had been in total secret and only the Russo-British-French negotiations were of public knowledge. Even Germany's allies such as Japan were shocked at the alliance and Russia's Communist sympathisers and other Jewish communities around the world could not understand how both Berlin and Moscow came together.

The fallout was controversial; Soviet propaganda stressed the fact that they had opposed the Nazi movement in Germany throughout the 1930's was now of little importance with Molotov handing an olive branch to the German people regarding fascism as a matter of taste. In effect he was saying that the far right in Germany was not as bad as once feared by the opposite left wing political class in the USSR. The Nazis for their part publically did a U-turn in its attitude toward Russia, even though Hitler still stuck to his principles set out in Mein Kampf in that a conflict with the Soviet

Union was still inevitable as part of Germany's 'destiny' to turn east. A complete break off of diplomatic relations between the Soviet Union and the west came about the very next day after the signing of the pact. French and British negotiators urgently requested a meeting with Kliment Voroshilov, the Russian military negotiator who informed them on the 25th that in light of the altered political situation, referring to the new alliance between Russia and Germany, no usefulness can be served in further conversation between their nations.

In Berlin, Hitler informed the British, through their ambassador in the German capital, that the Soviet pact alleviated the dilemma of a two front war; something that had worried the Germans and therefore changing the strategic situation from that which faced Germany throughout the First World War. Hitler then triumphantly, and somewhat pompously declared that Britain accept any other demands he has regarding Poland. However the British outfoxed him by signing a defence pact with the Polish. This guarantee of independence protected the sovereignty of Poland in the face of German military aggression. Hitler wanted to invade

Poland on the 26 August but in light of this surprise diplomatic move, he postponed. He knew the USSR would not interferer except under the terms of the territory changes of the secret protocol. Eventually at 04:45am on 1 September 1939, Germany finally, and fatefully, crossed the Polish frontiers.

Seeing that Hitler was not going to relent, Britain sent Germany an ultimatum to withdraw all forces out of Poland, scheduled to expire at 11am on Sunday 3 September. Once the deadline had passed, it was clear that Berlin had not cooperated; therefore Britain and by *de facto,* its empire were now in a state of war with Germany. By 5pm the same day France acted and it too was at war.

The USSR had not acted in accordance with the protocols of the Molotov-Ribbentrop Pact, and that is how Hitler wanted it. Eventually Germany and the Soviet Union would share a common border with each other for which an eventual titanic invasion could be launched when the time was right to realise the Nazi dream of a Greater German Reich in the east.

PART I – THE BLOODY ROAD TO STALINGRAD

"We have only to kick in the front door and the whole rotten Russian edifice will come tumbling down."
(Hitler 1941)

3

Barbarossa: Germany Assaults the Soviet Union

By 1941 the tide of the war had swung well in Germany's favour. There was no threat to the Third Reich in the east, indeed there was only one movement since Operation White (*Fall Weiss*), the invasion of Poland. After the initial Soviet incursion into Polish territory on the 17 September as per the Nazi-Soviet Pact secret protocol, a second one was put forward ceding Lithuania to the USSR, apart from the coastal region of Memel which was annexed directly into the East Prussian region of the Third Reich. These changes meant that just two years into the war, both Germany and the Soviet Union shared a border. Throughout 1940, Germany had astounding success both tactically and strategically. After Poland capitulated and the USSR fought Finland in the proxy conflict, the Winter War of 1939-40, a period of calm fell over Europe. This was known as the Phony War which was only shattered by the rapid German invasion and subsequent occupation of both Denmark and Norway beginning on 9 April. Just over four weeks later, Hitler ended the Phony War status for good by launching his long anticipated invasion of the West, Operation *Fall Gelb*, Case Yellow, 5th version known as Sicklestroke. Scheduled for 10 May to late June, the Germans overran Holland, Belgium, Luxembourg and perhaps most satisfactorily, France. The British Expeditionary Force were comprehensively routed and cornered at the small port of Dunkirk, forcing them into a humiliating retreat along with some of the French 1st Army. As a result of utter allied confusion and incompetence in the west, the rest of France now lay naked in front of the Nazis. By the 22 June 1940, the Germans were in Paris and the result was inevitable; France capitulated. By July and August 1940 and with virtually all of northern and western Europe under German control, a hastily thought out invasion campaign of the British

Isles, Operation *Seelowe* (Sealion) was only thwarted by a badly fought aerial campaign known as the Battle of Britain through to September and October. The sheer stubbornness of the British to come to terms while facing insurmountable odds ensured the United Kingdom boldly continuing as a very irritable thorn in Hitler's side for the coming future. In addition to Sealion, other proposed German invasion plans at this time included Operation *Tannenbaum* (Fir Tree), the planned invasion of Switzerland and Operation *Fall Grun* (Green) The invasion and occupation of the Republic of Ireland. Both were neutral counties, something the Nazis had no respect for. As early as the summer of 1940, Germany began plans for a forthcoming war against the Soviet Union and several plans were drawn up. Knowing that there was no real threat from Britain at this time, Hitler's critical timetable rushed him into his long cherished plan to expand east as prophesised in Mein Kampf. One of these plans, initially called Operation *Otto*, delivered on 5 December, was feasible but flawed. The plan relied on a huge simultaneous attack across three huge army groups, Army Group North, under the command of Field Marshal Ritter von Leeb, Army Group Centre under Field Marshal Fedor von Bock and Army Group South under command of Field Marshal Gerd von Rundstedt. Army Group North was to be launched from East Prussia and overrun the Baltic States and take Leningrad. Army Group Centre was to launch from northern Poland and drive through Minsk, Smolensk and eventually to assault Moscow itself. Army Group South, by far the biggest because the greatest Russian resistance was to be expected there due to the economic riches of the Ukraine (some of the most fertile lands in the Soviet Union) was based in southern Poland and the Balkans. Their objective was to take the Ukraine along with the key cities of Kiev and Kharkov. The main problem was in the centre. Facing von Bock was a huge natural obstacle, the Pripet Marshes close to the town of Pripyat straddling the Belorussian SSR and north Ukrainian SSR. This huge boggy area was deemed unsuitable for tanks, no good for rapid Blitzkrieg. If Army Group Centre was to advance across it, they would soon be slowed down, allowing too much time for a Soviet response. The answer was a small variant, in Otto. Army groups North and South were to carry on as planned, but Army Group Centre instead was to split and advance eastwards either side of the Pripet Marshes, encircling huge pockets of Soviet forces. Army Group Centre would then regroup at Minsk, an important road and rail junction before splitting again, this time pocketing and destroying more Red Army divisions, and encircling Smolensk. From them on, it would thrust eastward as a single group, converging on Moscow for the final battle. The variant to Operation Otto was called Operation *Barbarossa*, which was signed off and approved by Hitler on the 18 December 1940 scheduled for a start date of the 15 May 1941. Throughout the first few months preparations began, but the original start date had to be postponed due to developments in the Balkans. Fascist Italy under the stewardship of the dictator Benito Mussolini, who long sought a 'new Roman Empire', tried to assault Greece from Albania whom he had annexed in 1939. The assault was disastrous as the Greeks had counter attacked and conquered a quarter of Albania, thus prompting the intervention of Hitler. In May 1941, Axis satellite countries Romania and Bulgaria allowed passage for German troops but Yugoslavia refused to join in. Hitler therefore had to divert forces to invade Yugoslavia and Greece to save his Italian ally. This meant postponing the start date for Barbarossa until the 22 June 1941, some 38 days later. Finally after months of military and logistical build-up in the eastern border regions, at 03:15am on the 22nd, the code word 'DORTMUND' was issued signalling the start of the operation. Stalin, although concerned at the massive deployment of German and Axis forces along his border did not want to aggravate Hitler. He knew the Soviet Union would possibly go to war with Nazi Germany, but ideally not before 1942. It was not to be; German soldiers began murdering Soviet border guards prior to the invasion as a massive artillery barrage along a 2000 mile front, from the Black Sea to the Baltic fell upon the Russian defenders. Followed by Luftwaffe attacks against Soviet targets, the German forces, spearheaded by the panzer tanks went in. The initial frontier battles lasted until the 3 July with the Wehrmacht gaining the upper hand as they poured across the demarcation line that carved up Poland less than two years earlier.

Army Group North with strength of 600 tanks crossed the Neman and Dugava rivers and headed toward Leningrad. Four days of fighting after the Russians counter attacked with a force of 300 tanks and the Germans were superior over the poorly supplied Red Army. As the advance through the Baltic States continued anti-Soviet uprisings in Lithuania began. 30,000 people rebelled against the Red Army along with Lithuanian elements in the Soviet forces themselves. Dissent continued as the Germans reached Estonia as the population there rose up against the Russians as the main bulk of Army Group North approached the Luga River, within striking distance of Leningrad. By now the panzer groups had covered an impressive distance in a very short time prompting Hitler to order the tanks to halt to allow the infantry divisions to catch up, a similar situation to when the Germans smashed through France in 1940. The delay lasted one week, ample enough time for the Soviets to build up defensive positions on the Luga River and in Leningrad itself. It would prove to be the beginning of a very long siege of the city. In the middle, Army Group Centre attacked and encircled four Russian armies in a salient centred on Bialystok. Pocketing the massive Red Army forces, both panzer wings circumvented the Pripet Marshes crossing the River Neman on the northern flank and the Bug River in the south. This closed a trap on the defending Soviet 3rd, 4th, 10th and 11th armies at Bialystok and cut off their retreat further east. Capturing Minsk, the capital of the Belorussian SSR on the 27 June, more Soviet defenders were encircled and destroyed in the Minsk region as Army Group Centre reached the Dnieper and Dvina Rivers by the 3 July. Hitler believed incorrectly that the Red Army would be crushed by this point as it was thought to lay west of these rivers, but the Germans encountered more resistance as they were to split again; meeting a further five more Soviet armies. Encircling them, Army Group Centre managed to pocket and destroy three of these, the 16th, 19th and 20th armies. The other two, the 21st and 22nd escaped with severe damage as the Germans engaged the Russians around Smolensk commencing in early July. The fortunes of Army Group South however were different. Here the Germans met stiffer resistance as the Soviet command in this sector reacted quicker and so their progress suffered considerably. On the 26 June, 600 tanks of the 1st Panzer assaulted the eastern Ukraine with the objective of taking Brody close to the city of Lviv. The Red Army responded with a counter attack consisting of 1000 tanks, by far the greatest Russian assault. The result was a four day battle in the Lviv Oblast area that was one of the most bitterly contested of the Eastern Front. The Germans won out, but sustained heavy casualties on 1st Panzer. From now on, the Russians would only have enough strength to mount a defensive stance with a focus on a gradual withdrawal. This policy meant that the whole of the Western half of the Ukraine fell easily under German occupation, but was deemed an acceptable sacrifice as it drew resources away from the thrust toward Moscow, delaying the Nazis by 11 weeks. By the 3 July the panzers of Army Group Centre were now reinforced by infantry who had by now caught up and Hitler authorised a resumption of the drive eastwards. However summer rains further impeded progress allowing time for the Russians to better organise their defences. Up until now, Operation Barbarossa had been going like clockwork but now the Germans were coming up against the elements as well as stiffer opposition. To further compound matters, the Red Army staged a large counterattack against Army Group Centre whose ultimate objective was the city of Smolensk before the capital. The Russians counterattacked with 700 tanks but were eventually defeated by the Germans with the help of the Luftwaffe who had total dominance over the Red Air Force. The 2nd Panzer Army approached Smolensk from the south after forging the Dnieper while the 3rd Panzer closed in from the north following the failed Soviet assault. The advances from both directions would continue until the 26 July when the encirclement was complete, trapping 300,000 Red Army soldiers. However the pocket took a further ten days to destroy as a further 100,000 Russians escaped to the east, and Moscow. By now it was becoming disturbingly clear that the Russian strength had been massively underestimated by the General Staff in Berlin and this was logistically clear when the Germans began to run out of the supplies they had initially stockpiled for the operation. Resupply had to be a priority now so the

German strategy had to change; large numbers of Russian troops had managed to escape the huge encirclement battles that had dominated the campaign so far, so Hitler changed the goal. He now believed that a country as vast as the Soviet Union could only be defeated economically, in essence destroying their industrial base thus rendering them impotent and incapable of continuing the war. The logic was that if the Russians could not manufacture anything, then they would have nothing to fight with. Hitler's meddling horrified the Field Marshals. Up until now Barbarossa was on time and on schedule despite the supple concerns and the increased resistance, the Germans were on target to reach Moscow by November 1941. Army Group Centre was to be diverted first to the north to help with the rapid capture of Leningrad and a link up with the Finns who were also participating in the invasion. In addition to this elements of Army Group Centre were to be deployed across to help Army Group South in the assault on the Ukrainian industrial city of Kharkov. The German commanders themselves argued that Moscow should be a priority given that the bulk of the Russian armies were in that region as well the capital being the central hub for the USSR's transportation, communication and arms manufacture. Despite the obvious psychological blow to the Russians, Hitler was determined and issued direct orders that bypassed the Field Marshals, to swing the tanks north and south, stalling the drive on Moscow by early August. Back in the south, the Germans were within a few kilometres of Kiev, a position they had reached since mid-July. 1st Panzer in tandem with the German 17th Army struck south and east respectively, trapping the Russian 6th and 12th armies on the 15 July in Uman in central Ukraine. The Germans attacked the pocket, eliminating it by the 8 August, before crossing the Dnieper River further north. Meanwhile reinforcements from Army Group Centre in the form of 2nd Panzer crossed the River Desna along with the German 2nd Army; this manoeuvre trapped four more Soviet armies and elements of two more. In the north, at Leningrad, the 4th Panzer were themselves reinforced by units from Army Group Centre and in doing so broke through Russian defences on the 8 August. Advances from the northeast by the 16th Army and from the west the 18th Army cleared Estonia. By the end of August the Germans had advanced to within 30 miles of Leningrad while the Finns had pushed south to the old border before the Winter War. Leningrad was now totally under siege as Hitler ordered the complete destruction of the city which Army Group North tried to do on the 9 September. By the 19th the Germans were within 7 miles of the city but the advance had been costly in terms of lives lost. As a result Hitler eventually lost patience with this tactic and instead ordered that Leningrad should itself be sieged and its population starved. As forces were diverted from the middle, Army Group Centre remained largely static during the summer months. This meant that they were vulnerable to Soviet counterattacks in the Yelnya region just southeast of Smolensk. Here the Red Army attacked a 30 mile bulge in the Russian lines, inflicting Germany's first defeat during the Barbarossa campaign. It was enough for Hitler to turn the attention back to the centre, drawing the 3rd and 4th Panzers to break away from Leningrad and head south to prepare for a resumption of the drive on Moscow. In the south, the drive required operations around Kiev to be concluded as fast as possible. The Germans encircled Kiev and the surrounding Soviet forces by the 16 September as they pounded them with tanks and artillery barrages in a savage battle lasting until the 26th. The supposed final act of Barbarossa, the drive to Moscow commenced on the 2 October 1941. Named Operation *Typhoon* this was meant to be the last push to finally break the back of the Soviet Union and achieve victory in the east. After the battles around Kiev, the Red Army was now numerically inferior to the German Wehrmacht, and was now taking on a defensive stance in front of Army Group Centre whose first strike took the city of Oryol before pushing on and taking Bryansk. This move encircled the Soviet 3rd and 13th armies while further north the 3rd and 4th Panzer assaulted Vyazma. The battle here was particularly vicious as the Germans surrounded a further four Russian armies, the 19th, 20th, 24th and 32nd. This pocketing effectively destroyed Moscow's first line of defence and left the Russians with a mere 90,000 troops accompanied by just 150 tanks left to hold Moscow. Confident in victory, the Germans announced the pending capture of the Russian capital which fuelled the belief around the world of an imminent Soviet collapse. Advances east continued and by the 13 October the Germans were within 90 miles of Moscow. Panic set in the population, forcing Stalin to declare martial law upon the city. Nobody was allowed to leave; everyone was expected to do their bit in patriotic duty. Even though victory seemed achievable, there was one thing the Germans could not control, the weather. Since the beginning of October, around the time of the start of Typhoon, the Russian winter broke early, deteriorating the weather considerably and turning the roads into muddy quagmires. These atrocious conditions dramatically slowed the German advance to as little as 2 miles per day. Because of the slow progress, the supply of the troops became an ever increasing burden, rapidly deteriorating as time went on. It forced the Germans to pause to allow for the divisions to reorganise in front of massively stretched supply lines. In contrast, the Russians, who as they retreated eastwards had shorter and shorter supply lines, were far better organised than their German opponents. The Red Army consolidated their positions and organised a total of 11 new armies which included for the first time in this theatre, Siberian troops in reserve. Freshly redeployed from the Far East where the threat from the Japanese had rescinded; and with them came 1000 tanks and aircraft. By now the Germans who were approaching the limit of their endurance were nearing total exhaustion. But by the 15 November the dropping temperatures hardened the churned up ground allowing them to resume the drive toward Moscow. The Germans were closing in and wanted to let the 3rd and 4th Panzer armies cross the Moscow Canal in a bid to encircle the Russian capital from the north. 2nd Panzer assaulted the industrial city of Tula, 120 miles south of Moscow before closing in, but as the Russian resistance reacted, the 4th Army hit the centre of the Red Army defence. Fighting continued for the next 14 days with the Germans making slow but steady progress on the Moscow approaches despite worsening fuel and supply stocks and this meant that 2nd Panzer was being held in the south. On the 22 November Fresh Siberian units along with elements of the Soviet 49th and 50th armies counterattacked the German 2nd Panzer inflicting a defeat on them. 4th Panzer in the north pushed the Soviets back and crossed the Moscow Canal to begin the encirclement of the Russian capital. By the 2 December, German infantry of the 4th Army, the 258th Division pushed toward the outer perimeters of Moscow to the town of Khimki, just 5 miles west. At this point forward elements were only just 15 miles from the Kremlin, the Moskva River and Red Square itself. German soldiers could actually see the spires of the Kremlin on the horizon; the prize was tantalisingly close, but by now the first winter blizzards had begun. The Germans had captured the bridge in Khimki over the Moscow-Volga Canal and the local railway station, but this point marked the furthest eastern extent of the advance. Because Hitler had believed the Germans would defeat the Soviet Union in just six months, before the tenacity of the Soviet resistance had been realised, the Wehrmacht had not been equipped for winter warfare. Guns and sights froze in by now sub-zero temperatures and other equipment seized almost instantly. The bad weather also grounded the Luftwaffe, so the German ground forces literally had no protective air cover and the Russians exploited this. On the 5 December the Soviets launched a huge counterattack consisting of over 500,000 men, some elite Siberian units as well as other armies. The attack was too much for the Germans and their allies; overwhelmed. They were expelled from the Moscow region and driven back along the Soviet line called the 'Kalinin Front' and drove the Germans out of several cities around the capital. The counterattacks continued in temperatures as low as -42 degrees Centigrade throughout December 1941 and into January 1942. By the time the line had steadied, the Russians had pushed the Germans out of the Moscow region, a total of 155 miles back. Hitler's response was to move 800,000 men from Western Europe to the eastern front as well as dismissing a number of senior officers. By January it was now clear that Operation Typhoon, and with it the wider Operation Barbarossa objective to defeat the USSR had failed. It was not until the summer months that the next big offensive in the east would be launched by the Germans and their axis allies, the drive into southern Russia.

4

1942 Summer Offensive: Case Blue: Hitler's Thirst for Russian Oil

Case *Blau* (Blue) was Germany's plan to move into southern Russia during the summer of 1942. Later renamed Operation *Braunschweig*, it was intended as a continuation of the failed Operation Barbarossa the previous year. Issued by Fuhrer Directive No. 45, it was a strategic offensive since the Soviet Union was still in the war despite the large areas of land and resources captured by the Germans during the 1941 invasion. The ultimate goal of Case Blue was to finally knock the USSR out of the war for good by assaulting the Soviet Union's economic base for oil. Broadly speaking it involved a massive offensive into southern Russia aimed at the rich oilfields in the border regions with Persia (modern day

Iran), along a mountainous range titled the Caucasus. This formed a natural barrier between the Black Sea to the west and the Caspian Sea to the east, but was a central production for cotton and grain as well as heavy agriculture. The real prize was the oilfields in this region of which there were two, Maykop in the west and Grozny further east.

However further south, beyond the Caucasus were the heavily populated, highly industrialised Soviet republics of Armenia, Azerbaijan and Georgia. These were the true riches that the Germans wanted, being that they contained some of the largest oilfields in the world. The Azerbaijani capital, Baku, alone produced 24 million tons per year, accounting for as much as 80% of the Soviet Union's total oil output. On a broader economic footing, the Caucasus were also good stockpiles of peat and coal as well as other deposits such as Manganese ore for which 1.5 million tonnes cold be mined per year. Sugar beets, sunflower seeds, corn and wheat were also farmed in the south, making this part of the USSR vitally important for any side that had military control of the region. This made it very attractive to Hitler to keep the German war effort supplied not only along the eastern front, but also elsewhere in occupied Europe. Out of all the resources, oil was by far the most needed to keep the German panzer columns moving for any future offensive against Moscow or elsewhere and it was the Caucasus oilfields that caught Hitler's attention. By 1942, Germany was consuming 3 million tonnes of oil annually, but it was a resource that it lacked badly. 85% of Germany's oil was imported from countries such as Persia, the United States and South America. This arrangement changed once war had broken out in September 1939 when the British Royal Navy blockaded Germany, preventing her from importing oil from the Americas or Asia. This left Hitler with only one reliable outside source of crude oil, the axis satellite country of Romania which was rich thanks to oilfields such as the ones at Ploesti. The only other source of Germany's oil was to manufacture it within the state synthetically from coal. Oil was always going to be the weak resource and by December 1941, thanks to the occupation of the West the previous year and by massive thrusts into the Soviet Union during Barbarossa, Germany by now had almost exhausted its own supply. By the end of 1941, only 25% of Germany's oil was produced synthetically, with a massive 75% imported directly from Romania and this posed a dangerous situation for Hitler. Well aware of the possibility of allied air attacks on Romania only served to compound the problem of Germany's own declining fuel supply. Therefore the economic benefits of a strike into southern Russia were validated not only by the need for a new materials source, but to protect Germany's main economic ally in Romania. This was a vital requirement if Germany was to continue the prolonged war against its enemies. By 1942, Britain and its empire (such as Australia, Canada, India, New Zealand), the United States, a vast industrial powerhouse, and the Soviet Union were all against the Third Reich as well as other 'free' nations such as the French, Poles, Czechs and the Dutch. In 1939, Hitler wanted ideally a war in the east, but in the space of two and a half years his Germany was now fighting a dreaded war on two fronts against the largest empire in the world, the largest industrial power on earth and the largest army in Communist Russia. The necessity for increased oil and other resources had become a vital as well as strategic target for Hitler.

But by December of 1941, at the time Barbarossa was stalling due to the disasters at Moscow, Romania warned Germany that it too could not keep up with the demands. Bucharest warned Berlin that its own stockpiles were itself becoming exhausted. Therefore as the war became more global with the entry of Japan in the Far East after the attack on Pearl Harbour and the subsequent declaration of war on the USA by Hitler in support, the Soviet oilfields became ever more important to Germany's armed forces as well as her industry since by 1942 the Axis powers were beginning to experience serious shortages.

5

The Axis Order of Battle

Assembling forces for Case Blue, the entire responsibility of the forthcoming offensive fell to Army Group South. Intended to be conducted across the Russian steppe and the Germans committed 1,000,000 troops with a further 300,000 Axis allies in support. Italians, Romanians and Bulgarians formed the bulk of these swelling the total Axis strength to 1.3 million ready for the drive east.

To support the infantry 1,900 tanks stood ready to form the spearhead of the thrust accompanied by 1,610 aircraft of the Luftwaffe in aerial support. Army Group South was eventually split into two vast groups during the offensive; Army Group A commanded by Field Marshall Wilhelm List whose orders were to take Rostov prior to advancing into the Caucasus. List was a capable commander who began the war in command of the 14th Army and was based in Slovakia. He played active roles in Poland, France and Greece before being placed in overall command of Army Group A. Under his command List could call upon the First Panzer Army, the Seventeenth Army and the Eleventh Army. The Romanian contingent came from the Third Army in support. Army Group B was under the overall command of Field Marshall Maximilian von Weichs. A veteran of the Polish and French campaigns, Weichs was also had experience of previous engagements elsewhere on the Eastern Front. These included battles in Kiev, Smolensk and Bryansk. Weichs was charged with leading Army Group B toward the Volga and so had more armies at his disposal. These included the infantry of the Second Army and the prized Sixth Army, who had the prestigious distinction of capturing and triumphantly marching though Paris just two years earlier. Armour support came from the Fourth Panzer Army with Axis satellites support came from the Fourth Romanian Army and the Italian Eighth Army.

Air support for the whole operation came from Luftflotte 4 under the control of the Austrian Commander Alexander Lohr. Luftflotte 4 could call upon the 8th Air Corps (*Fliegerkorps VIII*) under Wolfram Freiherr von Richthofen and the 4th Air Corps (*Fliegerkorps IV*) under Alfred Keller.

Initially the German plan of attack was to be in three stages: Blau I consisted of the Fourth Panzer Army under the command of Hermann Hoth accompanied by the Second Army and supported by the Second Hungarian Army would all thrust forward between Kursk and Voronezh, pushing forward forming the northernmost flank of the advance toward the Volga. Blau II involved the Sixth Army, commanded by General Friedrich Paulus, advancing from Kharkov in eastern Ukraine, following parallel to Fourth Panzer and head directly for the industrial city of Stalingrad, and the Volga. Finally Blau III would signal the First Panzer Army to move south toward the lower Don River supported by the Seventeenth Army and the Romanian Fourth Army in the west and east respectively. Their objectives were the oilfields themselves at Maykop, Baku and Grozny.

The Germans hoped these three stages would result in massive encirclements of Russian forces facing them in the south.

6

Standing Ground – The Soviet Defenders

The Russian high command opposing the Axis drive was beset with confusion. Intelligence was relatively unclear as to what direction an impending German led 1942 summer offensive would take. However events would take a turn when a German officer called Joachim Reichel was shot down while undertaking a reconnaissance mission over territory east of Kharkov. Major Reichel was the chief of operations for the 23rd Panzer Division and just happened to have in his possession maps outlining plans for Case Blue. Immediately handed to the Soviet high command in Moscow, they were not exploited as Stalin, ever suspicious and convinced the German strategic goal for 1942 still to be Moscow, dismissed the plans as fake. His reasoning for this was because of a large German deception plan termed *Fall Kreml*, or Operation Kremlin designed to divert Soviet forces away from the southern sector by assaulting Moscow at the earliest opportunity. The Russians believed that Moscow was a more important target, (something that the Germans wanted them to swallow) and that Moscow was still the most viable strategic target rather than the economic south. To consolidate Soviet beliefs, the Germans even went as far as staging aerial reconnaissance flights over the Russian capital, providing maps of Moscow to ordinary soldiers and gaining intelligence on defences by interrogating prisoners of war.

The Russians fell for it and the bulk of their defending forces were deployed in the region, hundreds of miles further north than where they would actually be needed. However in the south total the Soviet strength was actually greater than the Axis armies, fielding 2.7 million men both in front line and reserve supported by 3720 tanks and approximately 1671 aircraft of the Red Air Force. Strategically there were deployed over four fronts. The first army group was called the Bryansk Front and composed the 40th, 48th, 3rd and 13th armies supported by the 5th Tank Army and 2nd Air Amy. The second group was called the Southwestern Front. This massive force, commanded by Marshal Timoshenko was comprised of the 6th, 21st, 38th and 40th Armies. By 1942 this front was broken up and eventually redeployed as the Stalingrad Front with elements absorbed into the third group, the Southern Front. This army group was subjected to a reorganisation with some reserve formations transferring to the Stalingrad sector to form the 62nd, 63rd and 64th armies at the heart of the Stalingrad Front. The final group was called the North Caucasian Front under the direct command of Marshal Semyon Budyonny. It was composed of elements from the now disbanded Crimean Front and eventually reinforcements from the Southern Front after parts of it transferred to Stalingrad. The Russian defence was subjected to a lot of reorganisation and changes to reflect the pressure and advances of the Axis invaders. Therefore formation, reorganisation and disbanding was a necessity to make the Soviet Defence as elastic as possible.

7

Axis Charge into Southern Russia

Case Blue, the German summer offensive drive to the Volga, Stalingrad and the Caucasian oilfields commenced properly on the 28 July 1942. It began by 4th Panzer driving toward the city of Voronezh causing Russian panic and a hasty retreat. The Germans exploited this, using the opportunity of Blitzkrieg to advance rapidly and making the most of Soviet chaos. Effective air support provided a measure of control of the skies above the offensive routes. The Luftwaffe totally dominated the Red Air Force gaining air superiority rather quickly through direct dogfights between German and Russian planes or through interdiction operations: the strategic bombing of airfields, and Soviet defence positions. The role of the Luftwaffe here was to fly ahead of the tanks and engage any Russian response ahead of the advance and from the air. This effective coordination and deployment strength was noticed by the command of the Bryansk Front as their divisions were pounded from aerial attacks, something which the Russians could not hope to match in either strength or accuracy. Inside the first month, the Soviets had lost a total of 783 aircraft compared to just 175 suffered by the Germans.

By 5 July the 4th Panzer reached the Don River close to Voronezh and was engaged in battle to capture the city. In defence the Russians had the 40th Army under the command of General Nikolai Fyodorovich. Hermann Hoth's 4th Panzer partly captured Voronezh a day later, occupying the Western suburbs, even though the Russians still believed Moscow was the intended objective. This caused them to rush reinforcements into the city in the shape of the 5th Tank Army and counter-attacked the northern flank of the German advance. Achieving minor successes, the Russians were eventually forced back to their starting positions by the 15 July as the German 6th Army followed 4th Panzer in the fight for the city. Once the occupation of Voronezh was complete by the 24 July, 6th Army turned south-east following the right hand bank of the Don River toward Stalingrad as directed by Operation Blue. However the Panzers were still in the city, held up for two days while supporting infantry divisions from Army Group South could catch up and secure the line against further Soviet counter-attacks. Although the attack on Voronezh was ultimately successful, there were divisions in the German high command especially between Hitler and Field Marshall von Bock, the commander of Army Group South since January 1942 following the sudden death of its previous commander, Walter von Reichenau. Von Bock and the Fuhrer argued over the next steps to be taken in the operation, which became quite intense. The situation was not helped by the continued efforts of Soviet counter-attacks and the delays to 4th Panzer, which caused Hitler to eventually, some might say, inevitably, lose his temper. In a rage, Hitler dismissed von Bock with immediate effect.

While Voronezh was still being secured in the north, on the 9 July Hitler made alterations to the Fuhrer Directive No. 45 and split Army Group South into the two smaller groups A and B. Army Group A under Wilhelm List as a replacement for von Bock was to strike south toward the oilfields. Army Group B under von Weichs was to protect the northern flank of Army Group A and head directly for Stalingrad. It was also expected to fend off any Russian counter-offensive from the north or east. However by the 11 July the Germans were once again experiencing problems with logistics given the vast areas that men and machines had to cross. This began to slow the advance, with the 6th Army experiencing fuel shortages. By the 20 July these fuel shortages were starting to affect more and more units, incurring a serious detrimental effect on the whole operation. Many units just could not carry out their orders. This prompted the Luftwaffe to aid in supplying the army from the air with the use of Junkers Ju52 transport planes. The air force had experience in this, having performed similar operations in Norway and the west in 1940 and during Barbarossa itself in 1941.

The practicality on the ground for the troops was that even with as much as 200 tons of supplies being flown in per day, some vehicles with high fuel consumption had to be abandoned or even fuel recovered from damaged equipment to keep the army going across the vast Russian steppe. This was a dangerous practice because it left some units seriously under-equipped in fighting vehicles, despite the coordinated effort between Army and the Luftwaffe. It resulted in the dismissal of Alexander Lohr as commander of Luftflotte 4 to be replaced by the commander of the 8th Air Corps, Wolfram von Richthofen.

8

Army Group A: Operation Edelweiss: Smashing into the Caucasus

For the drive south toward the Caucasus, codenamed Operation Edelweiss, the Axis summoned 167,000 troops, 1,130 tanks, 4,540 field guns and 15,000 specialist oil workers all supported by 1000 aircraft of the Luftwaffe 4th Air fleet. Heavily protected by Junkers Ju87 Stuka dive bombers, Army Group A punched through the front line and headed south, taking the Black Sea coastal town of Rostov by the 23 July. This was known as the 'Gateway to the Caucuses' and was easily reached with only token resistance thanks to the total air superiority of the Luftwaffe. However, further north, the 6th Army's progress was beginning to stall on the way to Stalingrad. This prompted Hitler to transfer the 4th Panzer back to the Volga and under the control of Army Group B, wasting precious time and resources in doing so. The Don River was crossed by the 25 July which marked the point where Army Group A could begin to manoeuvre. Once south of the crossing, they fanned out across a broad 200 mile front heading roughly toward the eastern coastline of the Black Sea beyond the Sea of Azov. The German 17th Army along with the 11th Army and the Romanian 3rd Army advanced south west toward the coast while 1st Panzer struck southeast. The German armour columns proceeded through the Soviet lines with ease, utilising the large open spaces of the region, a stark contrast to the fortunes of the 17th Army which was facing stiffer Russian resistance thus impeding, but not halting their advance. The advances continued and by the 29 July, the Germans finally managed to cut off the final rail link to the Caucuses from the rest of Russia. This panicked the Soviet high command and prompted Stalin to issue what would become a quite infamous order, the most poignant part being four little words: *"Not one step back!!"* By the 31 July, Army Group A had advanced 110 miles southeast of Rostov to the town of Salsk, part of the administrative centre of the Salsk district of the Rostov Oblast. By the 5 August 1942 Army Group A had reached the town of Voroshilovsk, now modern day Stavropol. Although the front of the advance was comprised primarily of light vehicles and reconnaissance forces since most of the heavy armour was further behind still suffering problems with logistics despite the Luftwaffe still flying in supplies. It was not until the 9 August that elements of Army Group A reached the foothills of the Caucasus at Maykop. By this time the Germans had, in two weeks, covered a distance of 200 miles into Soviet territory. The Maykop oilfields were the first to be seized before the nearby city of Pyatigorst fell. This was followed swiftly by the reaching of the Kuban River by the 12 August on which the city of Krasnodar lay further to the west, which the Germans managed to occupy. Army Group A entered the Caucasus Mountains with 10,000 troops of the 1st Mountain Division surrounding the highest peak, Mound Elbrus. Orders given to the Germans to climb the peak and plant the Swastika flag on its summit sent Hitler into a rage, threatening to court-marshal the commanding general who ordered the so-called 'stunt'. Overall the advance into the south by Army Group A had been broadly successful, yet the continued logistical issues remained a problem. Fuel still was the overriding concern for the divisions as they pushed forward, exacerbated by increasing supply lines since naval transport across the Black Sea was still not considered secure. Therefore the only option available to the Germans to get fuel to the front was either by air or by rail transport through Rostov. This meant that the Panzers spent intolerable amounts of time stood still as they had insufficient fuel supply to continue advancing. Even the supply trucks could not move as even they were very short or out of fuel; it was a real problem for the Axis who resorted, somewhat comically, to bringing up fuel on camels. By now the advance was beginning to stall. To compound matters, the focus of Operation Blue shifted to the region around Stalingrad, and since the priorities had changed, the German high command saw fit to weaken Army Group B by diverting some of its mobile forces under the command of 1st Panzer's Field Marshall Paul von Kleist to assist in the struggle further north. This included flak anti-air corps and a majority of Luftwaffe units, seriously depleting Army Group B's protection. These fears were realised as the Russians, who were in a general retreat on the ground, brought up air force units to attack the Germans using bombers to harass the enemy which was successful due to the lack of anti-aircraft cover and aerial support.

By the 28 August Soviet resistance hardened due to increasing strength of replacements and supplies coming from the local areas. This instilled a sense of patriotism in the defenders who fought with increasing tenacity which succeeded in slowing the Axis advance down. It seemed a push through the Caucuses and possibly beyond into Persia was destined to be a lot harder than anyone ever imagined.

9

The Oil Rich Regions

Further to the south east, the Axis forces headed toward their objectives at Baku and Grozny, both equally important petroleum oilfields. The Germans took more industrial refineries and oil installations either completely intact or with only minor damage as more oilfields fell into German hands. The Taman Peninsula opposite the Crimea was taken along with the city of Novorossik and its naval base by the beginning of September, allowing the Germans to continue advancing along the Black Sea coastline. However like in the Caucuses, Army Group A's advance was too halted outside Grozny itself once the Germans had taken the nearby town of Mozdok on the 25 August. In the rear areas, a guerrilla insurgency in the region of Chechnya rose up against the Soviets, putting up a fierce fight, assisted by German paratroopers whom the Chechen rebels saw as liberators; a situation not too dissimilar to that seen in the Baltic states during the early stages of Barbarossa. But even with this assistance, the mountain troops could not secure the ports of the Black Sea, compounded by the familiar logistical problems by vastly overstretched supply lines. This meant that the advance fell just short of Grozny itself. Russian resistance had once more tightened as they were determined to hold the oilfields here and fend off the Germans. Defending the installations were the 9th and 44th armies of the North Transcaucasian Front which was deployed ahead of the city to the north along the bank of the Terek River. Here the terrain was more rocky than expansive, ideally suited to an in depth defence. To make matters worse for the Germans, the advance had penetrated so far into Russian territory, the Luftwaffe were unable to support front line units. The result of this was that the Red Air Force in contrast was free at will to attack the Axis forces and their logistical supplies. Desperate to alleviate the situation, the Axis risked transporting reinforcements by ferrying them across the Black Sea from Romanian ports. A total of 30,605 men accompanied by 6,265 vehicles, and 31,254 horses arrived by naval transport by the 2 September. With additional forces, this allowed the German to complete the capture of most of the ports short of Novorossisk. The German assault only failed here because the Soviet 47th Army dug in with proper defences. It finally fell on the 10 September after a vicious battle. However Novorossisk marked Army Group A's final victory of Operation Edelweiss, the Russians still held the hills above the port just to the south along with strategic road links, preventing the Germans to break out. The Axis also could not take other coastal strongpoints further south, on the 25 September, the Soviets counter-attacked, the Romanians took particularly heavy punishment with their 3rd Mountain Division very nearly destroyed. This meant that the Axis forces only now had enough strength left to maintain a defensive line from further Russian assaults. The Axis progress was a little more positive further east. By the 1 September the Germans were moving toward the Caspian Sea coastal city of Astrakhan, reaching around halfway there as patrols continued to harass railways northeast of Grozny, something they had been doing since August. The focus of this interruption was the rail link between Astrakhan and the town of Kizlyar just off to the north east of Grozny. This position marked the furthest eastern advance of the German armies while further south, they stalled once again in the face of fierce Russian resistance in the air and on the ground before Grozny itself with 1st Panzer failing to capture the city. By the end of September and into the beginning of October a combination of this resistance and supply problems meant the Axis advance was hardly moving at all. However it was not all bad for the Axis. By the end of October the town of Nalchik, in the foothills of the Caucuses, was taken by the 13th Panzer Division and the Romanian 2nd Mountain Division; the prize was that in as little as two days, they captured as many as 10,000 Soviet soldiers. By the 5 November 1942 the Germans had advanced as far south as the region of North Ossetia taking the town of Alagir in the locality of the towns of Beslan and Malgobek. The region around these towns marked the furthest southern extent of the Axis forces as further north, the Germans tried to attack Grozny yet again only this time, frustratingly to be stopped just west of the city.

Because of the directions both army groups were now taking provided the very real opportunity that a strong Soviet counter assault could drive a wedge between both Army Groups A and B. This gap was only very lightly guarded by the Germans in the form of the 16th Motorized Infantry Division to defend the left most flank of 1st Panzer on the route toward Astrakhan. By November and the winter closing in, the Axis decided to take on a more defensive stance in readiness to resume operations in the spring of 1943.

10

The Luftwaffe Strikes

During the first half of October, as Army Group A was pushing through toward Grozny and the Caucasus regions, Hitler started to realise that the vital capture of the oilfields would probably not happen before the onset of the winter. This would mean that the forces would have to settle down for the duration in their positions. Upon this realisation, Hitler was adamant he had to deny the enemy those remaining oilfields and their installations, so ordered the Luftwaffe to inflict as much damage as possible upon them. He wanted the aerial offensive to start by the 14 October due to a priority toward the Stalingrad area. By the 10th, Luftflotte 4 bombers, every single one that was available to fly, was sent against the oilfields at Grozny, which could have delivered a massive blow if it wasn't for the air fleet to be in bad shape by this point. Under von Richthofen, 323 airworthy bombers out of total of 480 were available at the beginning of Operation Blue. By early October, out of a reduced bomber strength of 232, just 129 were now ready for combat. Even with this smaller force, they could still do an amount of damage as they hit the refineries causing huge plumes of thick black smoke rising 18,000 feet above the landscape. By the 12 October, the Luftwaffe bombed again with equally devastating results. Even with the level of bombing, if the Germans had attacked even more heavily the oilfields of both Grozny and Baku, this would have been a greater catastrophic loss to the Soviets both economically and strategically.

The bombings continued until the 19 November when Luftflotte 4 was forced to re-deploy further north to deal with the events at Stalingrad, relieving the southern oilfields from aerial attack. Grozny suffered heavy damage by air assaults, but other oilfields still remained intact due to them laying out of reach of the German ground units as well as the Luftwaffe. Grozny was only in range because it was attacked by the 4th Air Corps (Fliegerkorps IV) stationed close to the Terek River. The strategic situation was that economically, both the Maykop and Grozny fields only produced no more than 10% of the USSR's oil. The main fields at Baku were overwhelmingly the largest reserves, but were out of fighter range. Baku was in range of Luftwaffe bombers, but only in the most direct flight path beyond fighter cover meaning that the bombers would be at the mercy of the Russians fighters. Losses which the Luftwaffe could not afford to incur. By October, Russian air power in the region had strengthened enough to validate this argument. If the Germans had bombed Baku just two months earlier, the Soviet aerial strength was considerably weaker which would mean attacks on bomber formations would have been lacklustre at best. It was a very costly missed opportunity on the Axis part.

11

Army Group B: Operation Heron: The Drive East to the Volga

While Army Group A advanced south, Army Group B began its push east toward the Don and Volga Rivers, beginning on the 23 July 1942. From here on in, the Soviets began putting up increasingly stubborn resistance in the face of the advancing Germans thanks to their reorganised defence in the area. The Russians fielded two armies, the 62nd and the 64th making up the newly formed Stalingrad Front. Three days into the offensive, on the 26 July, the Soviet line was compromised by the 14th Panzer Corps who raced toward the Don River. In response, the Russians counter attacked General Friedrich Paulus' Sixth Army with two of their own tank armies, the 1st and 4th. Several attempts were made to push the Germans back and threaten the advance of 14th Panzer. However these proved unsuccessful due to the lack of experienced troops as 4th Panzer further south pushed forward against more Russian divisions, engaging and faring better against the 51st Army. The Panzers began to cross the Don, and on the 2 August, reached the nearby town of Kotelnikovo just 120 miles southwest of Stalingrad itself. Meanwhile further back, the Russian resistance hardened, even more convincing Paulus that the Sixth Army was not yet strong enough to force a crossing of the Don River alone. Needing reinforcements, Paulus halted the progress while 4th Panzer could break through north to reach them. By the 4 August, the Germans were still positioned only 60 miles west of Stalingrad as fighting along the western bank of the Don continued. The situation improved 6 days later, on the 10 August when the majority of the Russian resistance had been cleared from the western bank, although some pockets remained in the great bend of the Don River to harass the Germans by delaying their advance eastwards. The quality of the roads also did not help. The poor state of the road network contributed to the logistical problems suffered by Army Group B and the result of this was acute shortages of both fuel and ammunition. The lines, although stretched, were clogged by traffic jams thanks to the roads, seriously delaying the arrival of much needed supplies. Once again the Luftwaffe had to step in to alleviate the situation; as many as 300 Junkers Ju52 transport planes and even some bombers diverted from offensive operations were used to re-supply the forward units, enabling the Germans to continue their drive eastward. As time went on, the Russians were still holding out on the Don River. This forced the Germans to commit an increasing number of forces to deal with the situation and away from the front. This tactic left the German flanks dangerously undermanned, prompting the Russians to launch several counter-attacks against the northern flank of Army Group B along the whole front from Voronezh in the west and Stalingrad in the east. The counter offensive beginning on the 20 August, as two Soviet armies attacked 99 miles north-west of Stalingrad toward the town of Serafimovich, pushing the Italian 8th Army to fall back. Several other bridgeheads along the Don that were forced by the Russians were only opposed by the Italian 8th and Hungarian 2nd armies. These weaker Axis satellites would prove detrimental to the main German forces. By the 23 August, after a 21 day delay, the Sixth Army finally crossed the Don River. This freed up the rest of Army Group B to establish broader and more comprehensive defensive positions along the bends as Paulus pushed on toward Stalingrad, reaching the outer suburbs in the northern part of the city late in the day. The Romanians, Hungarians and Italians were deployed in defence 37 miles back from the city itself and this gave the Axis the means to assault the city from the air. On the ground the German intention was a two prolonged assault toward the city. Sixth Army was to advance from the town of Kalach and head north. In support, 4th Panzer was to come up from the south while the 14th Panzer Corps opened a narrow front between Paulus and the Volga at northern Stalingrad, while in the southern half of the city, heavy Soviet resistance repeatedly blocked 4th Panzer from making any further incursions. A further German attempt was tried on the 29 August with Field Marshall Hermann Hoth assaulting the centre of the defending Soviet

62ⁿᵈ Army. Taking the initiative, the Germans found themselves in the Russian rear areas, creating a bulge which provided the opportunity to encircle and cut off the 62ⁿᵈ Army. Seeing the chance, von Weichs ordered Paulus to wheel the Sixth Army round to complete the encirclement, but was themselves attacked by a strong Russian assault. This held Paulus up for three days, losing vital time and allowing the Russians to escape into the city itself despite the morale of the Red Army being at an all-time low. The disorganisation caused by the chaotic Soviet retreat left the outer defences of Stalingrad virtually intact.

By the 2 September, the Sixth Army resumed the attack into the city, linking up with 4ᵗʰ Panzer a day later. By the 12 September the preliminary battles around Stalingrad had finished as the Germans began entering into the urban areas, setting the scene for a vicious and bloody battle.

PART II – THE BATTLE FOR STALIN'S CITY

"And so the time for retreating is over. Not one step back!"
(Stalin 1942)

12

Stalingrad - The Beginning of the Assault

Stalingrad was a model Soviet city. Named after the Josef Stalin himself, it was seen as a centrepiece of Soviet Communism. This gave it a morbid fascination with Hitler who believed that the blow to the psyche of the Russian people would be intolerable if a city bearing their leaders name fell into German hands. When the Sixth Army reached Stalingrad on the 23rd, they were pursuing both the Soviet 62nd and 64th Armies as they fell into the city itself. Evan before the German advance had reached it the Russians had sufficient warning to move the economical assets away from the impending battle. This included grain and livestock but curiously the civilian population was not evacuated and therefore remained in the direct line of conflict. Even before the main battle had begun, there were severe food shortages thanks to preliminary attacks by the Luftwaffe on Russian supply ships in late July, making the Volga a dangerous crossing for any Soviet supplies being brought forward.

By late August and September, as the preliminary battles around the city were being completed in preparation for the Sixth Army to fight through the urban areas, the Luftwaffe opened the Battle of Stalingrad by heavily bombing the city. These air attacks conducted by Luftflotte 4 lasted throughout the late summer and autumn of 1942, and comprised some of the largest aerial formations of the entire Second World War. The effect was devastating; 1000 tonnes of bombs were dropped in total on Stalingrad, smashing large areas, and reducing many buildings to rubble. As in Moscow in 1941, civilians were prevented to leave under Stalin's orders, instead being put to work digging anti-tank trenches and other fortifications to bolster Stalingrad's defences. But this proved costly, a massive air raid on the 23 August created a huge firestorm, killing thousands and burning out large areas of the city, including 90% of the district of Voroshilovskiy. With most buildings now wrecked as the air assaults continued, crucially, the industrial base was at least left partially functioning. This meant that factories could continue to manufacture even as workers fought alongside the Red Army to repulse the German invaders in the city itself as the Sixth Army went in by 4pm.

The reason that the Germans enjoyed almost total air superiority over Stalingrad was that the Red Air Force was crushed by the Luftwaffe, losing over 200 aircraft by the end of August. Even as reinforcements were hurried in, the Russians could only depend on 192 airworthy planes, including just 52 fighters to take on the bombers. Even though the Soviets suffered appalling losses, they continued to throw reinforcements at the Germans but to no avail. The Luftwaffe was in absolute command in the skies over Stalingrad. One resident named Boris Kryzhanovsky summed up the bombing of his home city,

"After lunch on August 23 a colossal bombardment of the city began. The whole city was razed in just two days. The central district was destroyed first. We left for a refugee centre, on the next day, out house just wasn't there any longer."

Initially the heaviest defence of the city was entrusted upon the largely female volunteer force anti-aircraft units, namely the 1077th Anti-Aircraft Regiment. The training they received was for engaging air targets only and not for any ground units, even though the Russians, with strength of only 37 guns decided to attack the German armour themselves. Taking on the 16th Panzer Division, they matched them for a while until all guns were knocked out or completely overrun. Only then did the Germans discover that the Russians had been using female soldiers in the front lines. Women played a large, significant and important role in the battle of Stalingrad. As many as 75,000 females took part, manning anti-aircraft positions to engage both the Luftwaffe and the German panzers. It was also women who undertook the incredibly dangerous job of braving enemy fire to bring back the wounded to field hospitals where they also tended to the injured in nursing roles. In the front line positions, women took to manning mortars and machine guns as well as artillery spotters alongside the men and also matched their male comrades as snipers. Large scale female casualties though came from their role as telephone and radio operators. This was because women in this capacity were stationed in the front line command positions, which came under direct fire from the Germans.

Despite the role of females alongside their men folk in the defence of Stalingrad, the Red Army still suffered disorganization within the Soviet ranks. The secret service, the NKVD, a forerunner to the MVD which eventually became the KGB, organised militias in the city, groups of workers and civilians for participation in the battle. Often either poorly or even non-equipped, many people were sent defenceless into the fighting without any weapons at all. Although this obstacle inspired some ingenious ideas in the name of patriotic duty and in the face of desperation; one of Stalingrad's more productive industries, the tractor factory, workers utilised the machines to assemble tanks like the Soviet T-34 from parts, driving them, often unpainted straight into the front.

By the beginning of September, the Soviets could only reinforce existing Russian forces in Stalingrad due to the German advance by Paulus to the northern suburbs and to the south by Hoth's panzers. The only way to do it was to undertake the dangerous river crossing across the Volga under constant threat from air attack and shellfire. As the Sixth Army went in, during a second attempt on the 27 August and supported by the Croatian 369th Infantry Regiment, Stalin had to respond. Therefore he made Stalingrad a priority, rushing all available troops into the area, deploying them initially on the eastern bank of the Volga, crossing them by the river to reinforce the existing forces already desperately holding on inside the city. By the 5 September the Russians launched a huge counter attack against the 14th Panzer Corps with 150 tanks. It was ultimately beaten back thanks in large part to the air superiority by the Luftwaffe attacking Soviet artillery and defensive positions, destroying 30 of these tanks in the process. The coordinated assault by both ground and air ensured that the Soviets had no other choice but to withdraw by midday. The attack, although bitter, was brief, lasting only but a few hours.

Day after day the Luftwaffe continued to harass Soviet movements. The Russian 1st Guards, supported by the 24th Army launched a counter offensive with 106 tanks against the Germans just to the north-west of the city, at the town of Kotluban on the 18 September. The 8th Flying Corps of Luftflotte 4 assaulted the Soviet armour with Junkers Ju87 Stuka dive bombers in an attempt to hold them back, knocking out 41 in total. Supporting Soviet fighters were themselves pounced upon by Luftwaffe Messerschmitt Bf109 fighters, losing 77 to the Germans. The offensive at Kotluban failed ensuring that there were no Soviet initiatives in to the north. Within Stalingrad itself, the ruined city became terrain favouring the defenders. The Russian 13th Guards Rifle Division commanded by Lieutenant General Alexander Rodimtsev, along with the 64th and 62nd Armies formed their defences along houses and factories as strongpoints designed to hold off the Germans as long as possible.

Fighting between Friedrich Paulus' Sixth Army and the Soviet defenders was fierce. Every step of ground, every house, every room was contested in the most bitter of ways, exaggerated in part by the issue of Stalin's orders stating that soldiers must stand their ground whenever and wherever possible. Despite this the Germans were confident, as summed up by one Wehrmacht solder, Wilhelm Hoffman,

"Excellent news! Our forces have reached the Volga and taken part of the city. There are only two choices for the Russians. To the north, our forces are taking the city and reaching the Volga-but to the south, ill-fated Russian divisions continue to offer terrible resistance. These people must be fanatics..."

Indeed it must have seemed so. Any soldiers that retreated when not authorised to do so could expect to face a military tribunal-meaning either incarceration in a labour camp; or quite simply, death by execution. Indeed such was the Soviet ideological hatred of fascism, that any evidence of cowardice in the face of the enemy by Russian infantrymen would be met by bullets from their own side, from the political commissars. This degree of terror in the Red Army was intended to expel any defeatism in the morale of the Soviet troops; if they feared their masters more than the enemy they would be more inclined to fight when ordered. Stalin's 'Not one step back' Order 227 marked a change in the Soviet attitude that retreating further east was no longer an option. By 1942, the Red Army fought because it was forced to fight where it stood; both under orders from higher authorities and also in light of the geographical and economic position the USSR found itself in at this time. This ramped up the bitterness and desperation of the fighting and the result was that the Germans continued to suffer increasingly heavier casualties as they pushed deeper into Stalingrad.

13

Inner City Murder

As the 20,000 soldiers of the 62nd Army entrenched themselves into the city by the 12 September 1942, the Russians could only call upon 90 tanks, some of which were used as stationary turrets at strategic points, and 700 mortars for support. The German Sixth Army's initial plan of attack was to move and overrun the city quickly before any serious suburban fighting could develop, bogging down the forces. For this the Germans tried to assault Stalingrad in a three pronged attack, one infantry division went for the central railway station, another, the central landing stage on the Volga, and the third to take Mamayev Kurgan. This was a high ground overlooking the city itself and the river beyond and was a strategic point for anyone wishing to monitor and control movements of both sides throughout the battle. The Germans codenamed their assault on the city Operation *Hubertus*.

In response, the Soviets ferried in badly needed reinforcements across the Volga to try and hold the Germans back within the city. Suffering appalling casualties, the Russians launched a counter attack with 10,000 troops at Mamayev Kurgan and the main railway station. The 13th Guards Rifle Division was tasked with taking both objectives, but the fighting at the rail station was bitter. During the battle, it had changed hands from German to Russian and back to German control continuously as each side slaughtered each other. Within just six hours the railway station had changed hands a total of 14 times such was the ferocity of the fighting. Eventually for the time being the Russians finally managed to seize their objective, along with Mamayev Kurgan, where the Germans also put up fierce resistance. As a result of this, the 13th Guards Rifle Division had suffered 30% of its soldiers killed within the first 24 hours. So great were the Soviet losses that the average life expectancy of a Red Army officer sent into Stalingrad at this point was just *three* days. If you were an ordinary soldier, however, your chances of survival were even worse, just *one* day before you were expected to be killed. These losses could not be sustained by the Russians by the time the offensive had concluded, out of 10,000 Soviet troops originally committed to the counter offensive, just 320 had managed to survive. Such pitiful numbers meant that command was no longer possible and the following evening the 13th Guards Rifle Division had effectively ceased to exist such was the sacrifice to take both Mamayev Kurgan and the station. They had achieved what was asked of them, but they almost wiped themselves out in the process to the point where they could not constitute a single fighting unit. More evidence of Soviet tenacity was proven to the south of Stalingrad. Here was an installation vital to food processing constituting of silos and a large structure known as the Grain Elevator. General Paulus thought it an ideal spot for a memorial to celebrate the expected German victory at Stalingrad such was this economic symbol to the city. However it was occupied by Russian forces who in reality, were virtually cut off from supply. By the 17 September eighteen sailors of the 92nd Rifle Brigade managed to get through to the beleaguered men holding out under tank and Stuka bombardment. By dawn the next day, the Germans tried to get the Russians to surrender by approaching them in a tank, warning them that it would be useless to carry on and to get out otherwise the whole elevator would be bombed flat. The Soviets refused, telling the *"Fascists"* to *"Go to hell"*. As the Germans in their tank tried to retreat back to their lines, the Russians fired upon them with anti-tank weapons knocking it out, send a clear and defiant Soviet message. Throughout the 18 September, the Germans attacked the elevator ten times with armour and infantry from both the south and west. For the next 3 days the fighting became bitter. The grain that was stored caught fire, from pounding from shells and mortars creating intense heat and smoke, causing water to evaporate from the machine guns. To complicate matters, the wounded had nothing to drink. Ammunition was just as scarce forcing each defender to use their remaining bullets very carefully. Repeated attacks came one after the other as the

Luftwaffe circled overhead, reporting the Russian positions and directing fire accordingly. The Germans actually managed to enter the elevator from the western side as smoke and dust from shell shattered concrete clouded everybody's vision. Close quarters fighting and even hand to hand combat raged through the devastated floors Each attack was fended off under hot, dirty and intolerable conditions until there seemed to be nothing left; the Soviets running low on ammunition, tired and thirsty, decided to break out. The Germans moved in, expecting to find a large Red Army contingent holding out given the fanaticism of the resistance. They were in for a rude shock; once inside the huge structure, they found the Soviet dead, killed during the battles. They discovered only 40 bodies, surprising the Germans as to how hard this tiny number had fought.

Within Stalingrad itself, the Red Army employed the idea of holding on to as much ground in the city for as long as possible. This required turning whatever building or other structures into as strong a fortification as possible manned by small units of just 5 to 10 men. As the fighting continued the

Russians constantly had to ship fresh troops across the Volga to keep the 62nd Army resistance going, vital if the Germans overran a position, the Russians would still have the manpower to attempt to take it back. Even in street fighting conditions, the Germans still employed the Blitzkrieg doctrine of combined arms: coordination between infantry, artillery and aircraft; the trouble with this was that it relied heavily on supporting fire. This intensified the scale of the fighting, as experienced on the 21 September by another resident, Serafima Voronina,

"Two soldiers popped in today for a drink, so we asked them, 'will it end soon?' They said they didn't know-no other city has stood up to it as long as Stalingrad. Today, its 30 days since the bombardment began. Thirty days since we hid in this crack." The Soviets on the other hand, thanks to their fortifications, preferred to keep the front lines as close to the Germans as possible, keeping their forces tied up, reducing their supporting fire and slowing down their advance. This was exactly the bogging down of troops that Paulus wanted to avoid and it worked. The Russian commander of the Soviet 62nd Army

defending Stalingrad, and Paulus' opposite number was Lieutenant General Vasily Chuikov who described the tactic of keeping close to the Germans in one simple word, "Hugging." The result of these strategies was that everything was contested. Every building, every floor, even every room was mercilessly fought over. It was not uncommon for a typical building or ruin to be occupied by opposing forces on different floors; if the Soviets held the basement, the Germans might hold the ground floor. If the Russians held the second floor, the Germans would occupy the upper floors or attic. Every building, ruined residential areas, office blocks and basements therefore became a death trap. With tall buildings bombed out by earlier German assaults, Soviets and Nazis would fire at each other in holes in the floor or gaps in walls in desperate attempts to clear out the enemy room by room in close quarters urban combat. It was extremely dangerous; opposing soldiers could literally be just meters apart. Just deciding if or not to enter into an adjacent room could mean the difference between surviving or getting shot. The fighting even extended underground, into the sewer systems where men would kill each other in the most foul of conditions and inhospitable of places. All this led to the fighting at Stalingrad, as bitter as it was, being labelled by the Germans as the *Rattenkrieg* meaning 'Rat War'.

As the fighting became tougher, the politicians sought to galvanise both the people and the army in the ensuing struggle. Hitler gave one such speech to the crowds at the Berlin Sportspalast in the 30 September about both the battle and the wider campaign,

"The goal was: First, to take from the enemy his last big wheat regions. Second, to take from him the last remaining coal which can be made into coke. Third, to move up to his sources of oil, to take them, or at least to isolate them."

Here Hitler tried to justify to the German people the reasons for attacking Southern Russia. Arguing for economic benefit rather than a military strategic gain,

"Fifth, the attack was to be carried on to cut off his very last and greatest communication artery, namely the Volga. And here the goal set was the region between the bend of the Don and the Volga, and the locale set was that of Stalingrad, not because

this locality bears the name of Stalin-that is altogether a matter of indifference to us-but exclusively because this is a strategically important point. And since in general we realized that with the elimination for Russia of the Dnieper, Don, and Volga as communication lines about the same thing results for Russia or even worse, that would result for Germany if we should lose the Rhine, the Elbe, the Oder, or the Danube. For, on this gigantic river alone, the Volga, in six months about 30,000,000 tons of goods are shipped. This corresponds to a whole year's shipments on the Rhine."

Really? The name Stalingrad was a matter of indifference for the Germans? Stalingrad may have held very real strategic and industrial prestige, but as time wore on the psychological influence of the name would become an overriding feature to Hitler. So much so that there was a danger of the importance of Stalingrad causing negligence elsewhere along the front, even in the Caucuses where the main objectives of Operation Blue were supposed to lie. He continued,

"This is cut off and has been cut off now for some time. The occupation of Stalingrad,

which will also be carried through, will deepen this gigantic victory and strengthen it, and you can be sure that no human being will drive us out of this place later on."

For the German military, Stalingrad, strategically speaking was the lynchpin that the whole northern flank to resist any Russian assault was to be based on. But for Hitler himself, he was beginning to display signs that the city was all about military, personal, and ideological superiority over Stalin. Elsewhere battles across the city were becoming ever fiercer. The prominent hill, Manayev Kurgan was the scene for some of the bloodiest contests in the area, changing between Russians and German hands continuously as each side fought and killed mercilessly. In other areas, the Sixth Army was being held up by specific Soviet strongpoints. These were usually houses of other single buildings that provided adequate defence for Russians holding out against sustained resistance, often with great bravery. One such fortress was known as Pavlov's House. A four storey building that overlooked the Volga and the ground further back. It provided excellent views of the river bank and the surrounding areas, making it ideal for holding out and dominating the vicinity. On the night of the 27 September 1942 a small reconnaissance platoon led by Sargent Yakov Pavlov captured the tall structure from the occupying Germans. Immediately they set about turning it into a strongpoint, fortifying it with a surrounding minefield, and machine guns in the windows. Even with residents hiding in the basement, the defenders of Pavlov's House were not relieved for nearly eight weeks, holding out relentlessly against German assaults. Such was the tenacious defence of this strongpoint, Pavlov's House was known as a *Festung,* the German word for fortress on the Sixth Army's maps and with good reason. The Soviet commander in Stalingrad, Vasily Chuikov remarked that the Germans lost more men at Pavlov's House than they did capturing the whole of Paris in 1940.

Even with the carnage and the sheer stubbornness of the Red Army, the Germans pushed steadily through the rubble of the city, but painfully slowly. As the Sixth Army advanced, they did take some strategic positions but crucially the key crossing points at the Volga were just out of reach. A combination of Luftwaffe attacks, armour and artillery support were employed to help the infantry with varying success. This prompted the Germans use utilise one of their more interesting and deadly weapons, a massive artillery piece, oversized and running on rails. The rail gun named Dora was brought up into the area to hurl shells into Stalingrad and blast the Soviets out in response to the Russians deploying artillery batteries on the east side of the Volga. These pieces had been shelling the Germans in the city itself as counter-artillery or just as supporting bombardments for Soviet counter attacks. By now the fighting had degenerated to such a level that any tactical decisiveness had almost gone away; Stalingrad was now a battle of attrition. This bore a terrifying new aspect to the situation: sniper fire. The twisted metallic ruins of the industrial areas and the rubble strewn brick structures of the residential suburbs and city centre provided fertile ground for specialist snipers to move through. Targets were either officers or soldiers bringing up supplies, usually food and water to the forward positions. Moving through any open space could mean exposure in a sniper's crosshairs, and instant death. The psychological pressure of this terror on both sides was immense but for the Germans, they had to contest with the fear of a Soviet sniper called Vasily Zaytsev. Zaytsev was a skilled sharpshooter with his Mosin-Nagant rifle who amassed a total of 225 kills during the entire battle taking out supply runners and artillery spotters if possible.

Amongst all of this, military rank was no barrier to the strain exerted on both sides. Both leaders were feeling the stress and strain of such a violent battle. Vasily Chuikov experienced an outbreak of eczema which affected his hands, causing them to be completely bandaged. The German commander fared no better, Friedrich Paulus developed a tic in his left eye, which spread to affect the entire half of his face as both sides came to the reality of constant close combat.

On a wider political scale, for both Nazi and Soviet leaders, Stalingrad had a prestige beyond anything else. For Hitler, he desperately wanted to take the city, not only for strategic purposes as part of the wider Case Blue, but also as a psychological blow to the Soviet people. For Stalin himself, it would be an intolerable humiliation and a complete undermining of his authority if the city which bears his own name was to fall into the hands of his ideological enemy. Therefore he was prepared to throw everything into the defence of Stalingrad, even transferring reserves from the Moscow region as well as the Soviet Union's entire air force into the area. Anything to hold the Germans back; but the Sixth Army was not finished yet.

14

The Luftwaffe Strikes Again

By early October the Luftwaffe began operations to decisively knock out the Soviets in Stalingrad for good. On the 5th, Stuka dive bombers of Luftflotte 4 attacked Russian positions at the Tractor Factory completely annihilating several Red Army regiments in the vicinity. It was a tremendous outcome for the Germans which continued the next day, killing more officers of infantry regiments as a result of relentless air raids. On the 6 October the Russian 339th Infantry Regiment suffered particularly heavy losses from the Luftwaffe assaults. As the Soviets desperately held on against the Sixth Army, the Luftwaffe stepped up their air attacks on the Soviet positions situated on the western bank of the Volga. The German ground forces surrounded the industrial areas including the Stalingrad (named *Dzerzhinsky*) Tractor Factory throughout the month. Flying a total of 2000 missions on the 14 October alone, the Luftwaffe dropped 550 tonnes of bombs and high explosives on the Russians defending the factories. As the bombers concentrated on the industrial regions, Stukas went for the Soviet artillery on the eastern bank of the Volga, silencing them and preventing any more shelling of the ground forces as they fought their way closer to the river. This freed up the dive bombers to then turn their attention to the Russian shipping as the Red Army were still trying, desperately to ferry reinforcements into the narrowing Russian held areas. Things were looking extremely bleak for the Soviets; Chuikov's 62nd Army had now finally been cut in two as it looked like the Russians were going to lose the battle of Stalingrad. Their support was now dwindling as the Luftwaffe increasingly attacked troops and material supplies as they crossed the river. By now the Russians had their back to the Volga, occupying a narrow strip of land just 1 kilometre wide on the west bank. To the Russians, it looked like Stalingrad had been lost as the Germans held nine-tenths of the city. In support of this the Stukas flew over 1200 missions against the remaining elements of the 62nd Army to finally eliminate the Russian resistance inside the pockets but the steep banks of the Volga proved, mercifully to prove impenetrable to the Germans. By now the Nazi Swastika flag was being flown at various sites over the city in expected triumph. As October drew to a close and November began, the Luftwaffe enjoyed total air superiority over Stalingrad as the Soviet Air force was unable to mount daytime aerial operations. However this was not always good for the Germans; all this flying took its toll on the Luftwaffe aircraft. Originally with 1,600 airworthy planes, the dominance of the air reduced this to just 950 to police the skies over Stalingrad. The bombers had suffered the greatest reductions, having only 232 planes left to fly by November out of 480. Given these 'losses' the Red Air Force was still inferior in the quality of planes, but were actually building up their total strength to a point where they would actually be able to outnumber the Luftwaffe. For the Germans, even though the Luftwaffe was bombing the defenders pocketed in Stalingrad, the grand scheme of things had been lost in the fanaticism for control of the city. Air strength had been diverted away from supporting the forces in the drive for the Caucuses and the oilfields. This was Hitler's original grand objective both economically and strategically for Case Blue, but the preoccupation with Stalingrad proved too great. It was a fatal error. In contrast to the Luftwaffe, the Soviet bomber force had taken heavy losses since Germany invaded the Soviet Union and therefore could only fly at night safely. These night time raids were conducted over Stalingrad and further west, over the Don bend but due to the lack of strength and accuracy, bore little in the way of results. In the raids conducted between July and November 1942, negligible damage was inflicted on the Germans reducing the effectiveness of the Soviet raids to just a nuisance.

But this inequality was not to last, events were to take a turn thousands of miles away. By the 8 November a British and American landing at Algeria in North Africa took place in what was known as Operation Torch. This offensive was to squeeze Erwin Rommel's German Afrika Korps who had been chased out of Egypt by Bernard Montgomery's 8th Army the Desert Rats and across Libya since they were turned at the Battle of El Alamein. Torch was to allow the allies, which was the first engagement of the war for the Americans to race across Algeria and attack the Germans as they were held up in Tunisia, and finally force them out of the continent and back toward Sicily and Italy. In response to this new threat, the Germans withdrew vital elements of Luftflotte 4 at Stalingrad, re-deploying them to North Africa. This meant that the Luftwaffe found itself stretched from the Mediterranean to Southern Russia severely impacting its strength on the eastern front. The Luftwaffe had struck again, but this time at a cost one way or another. In contrast to the German problems, the introduction of the USA into the war meant that the USSR could tap into America's industrial strength. Like the UK receiving aid under Lend-Lease, the Soviet Union also began receiving material supplies from the United States under an extension of the program. In truth they had been receiving supplies from the UK since 1941 in the form of the arctic convoys, and by now the US boosted Russian defences, shipping as much as 45,000 tonnes of explosives and 230,000 tonnes of aviation fuel. The same day Operation Torch was commenced in Africa; German confidence was high given the perilous Russian situation. Hitler cheerfully commented reflecting this,

"I wanted to come to the Volga at a specific location at a specific city. By chance it carries the name of Stalin himself. So don't think I marched there for this reason – it could carry another name – but because there is a very important goal... this goal I wanted to take - and you know – we are very modest, we have it already.

There are only some very small places remaining. Now the others say 'why aren't they fighting faster?' Because I don't want to have a second Verdun there, I'd rather take it with small assault groups."

15

The German Flank is Exposed...

By now in the city itself, with all that the Germans had captured (nine-tenths) and the splitting of the 62nd Army, desperate reinforcements could no longer arrive. The Luftwaffe had taken their toll, but now the weather began to turn as winter approached. By November parts of the Volga began to freeze creating large ice flows on the water, preventing any ships from crossing. The remaining Russian defenders were now completely cut off, surrounded and on their own in the face of the enemy.

However resistance still stoically continued. The industrial regions in the northern sector of Stalingrad, particularly the 'Lazur' Chemical Factory, the Krasny Oktyabr (Red October) steel factory and the Krasnaya

Barrikady (Red Barricades) ordnance factory still held out against German attacks, but only just. As part of Operation Hubertus, the Germans tried desperately with pioneer troops to assault the administration building of Barrikady, known to them as the 'Red House' while elsewhere, on the 14th fighting still raged as the Germans captured two housing blocks on the eastern side of the plant which was counter attacked immediately by 150 Russian troops. The Germans gunned them down in a bid to successfully hold them off. Fighting continued on the ever important slopes of the high ground on Mamayev Kurgan, still contested even now. But now the Germans were virtually at the Volga, some troops even remarked that they could see Asia, meaning the eastern bank of the river even though this was not strictly true. European Russia extends further east to the Ural Mountains so technically they were still on the continent.

As the winter of 1942 began to set in, it was noticed by the Soviets that the Germans were not properly equipped for cold weather fighting. Most of them were redeployed in other areas of the southern sector on the eastern front and this prompted the Russians to conduct offensives between November and February. The Soviet Winter Campaign between 1942-43 which began in November and would continue until March in other sectors would eventually involve an additional 15 armies across several different areas.

In Stalingrad itself, the Winter Campaign was about to mark a massive shift in the fortunes of the battle. As the Germans hunkered down in their positions, the Russians prepared....

The Germans effectively sieged the Soviets tied up at the Volga. They had strength in Stalingrad itself but the overall strategic situation was rather precarious on the flanks. The Italian 8th Army, Hungarian 2nd Army and the Romanian 3rd and 4th Armies were tasked alongside the Germans with protecting Army Group B's flank. This front, straddling both the Volga and Don rivers faced north, the logical direction of a Soviet counter-attack should one come. However due to the continuing struggle in Stalingrad, the flanks had pressed their headquarters for reinforcements with little success. The Axis armies had a big responsibility; the Hungarians were charged with defending a

120 mile front from the left of the Italians, all the way to the east of Voronezh. The large spaces to which the 2nd Army had to fit into and defend meant that it had to be deployed very thinly indeed. In some places sectors just 2 kilometres wide only had a token defence, a single platoon at most. They were also badly equipped, with a serious lacking of anti-tank weapons. No good if the Soviets attacked in strength with armour.

The main problem was that the focus on Stalingrad and the desperate fighting inside it had gone on for months, so much so that Axis positions along the Don River had been seriously neglected in terms of supply and manpower. Because of this, a tactical aspect was overlooked resulting in a grave error of judgement. The Russians had not been cleared away from the eastern banks of the Don, meaning that if the Soviets wanted to launch a counter-offensive, these would be ideal staging areas. Therefore the Axis had a serious problem; the east bank of the Don to the north posed a very real threat to the flank of Army Group B.

It was no better to the south of Stalingrad. Facing any Soviet reserves on the east bank of the Volga were the solitary German 16th

Motorised Infantry accompanied by the Romanian 7th Army Corps. This light holding force was all that stood between the Russians and the Axis rear areas. Hitler's abnormal fixation with Stalingrad, Axis neglect and military incompetence created this precarious situation on the flanks of the city, and a tempting target for the Soviet high command…

16

The Russian Fight Back – Operation Uranus

By this stage of the operation, the Axis powers had worked themselves into a situation that could be exploited and that it was inevitable that the Soviets could try and take the initiative. By September 1942, the Russians decided to take the offensive back to Germany and its allies in an operation codenamed 'Uranus'.

Planning for Operation Uranus began that same month, as the Germans entered Stalingrad. Marshall Georgy Zhukov, hero of the Siege of Leningrad and the defence of Moscow travelled to the south to assess the dire situation. Reporting directly to Stalin upon his return to the Kremlin, he stated that the area badly needed reinforcements. He mentioned to another officer present at the meeting, General Aleksandr Vasilevsky that a radical solution was needed in the area which Stalin himself overheard. Breaking with habit, the Soviet leader decided not to have a direct hands-on approach to the situation and told both officers to work on a plan that would relieve Stalingrad once and for all. This plan would eventually become Operation Uranus. The overall objective was to take advantage of the positioning of the Axis by launching two huge thrusts to the north and south with the ultimate aim of creating a massive encirclement of the German Sixth Army, part of the 4th Panzer, as well as the 3rd and 4th Romanian armies in the process. In addition to Uranus, the Soviets also wanted to assault the Germans further south in the Caucuses as well as further north against Army Group Centre.

Taking advantage of the Germans inadequacy to prepare for the coming winter, the Russians planned to establish themselves opposite the weaker Axis flanks along the Don and Volga Rivers. Poor deployment along the front lines especially in southern Russia due to a stretching of the Axis (and the draining effect the fighting inside

Stalingrad had on the German forces), meant that weaker Romanian troops would be pitted against hardened Soviet tank armies and shock troops. This was extremely dangerous for the Axis as the Romanians in particular had no heavy equipment in the form of anti-tank weapons to deal with Soviet armour.

Because of the German advances under Operation Blue this had created vast front lines, the Axis forces found themselves covering areas greater than they comfortably could do with any effective depth. What weakened the front lines was the utter depletion in strength after months of bitter fighting inside and outside of Stalingrad of the German units, not helped by the military command's decision to transfer several divisions from the USSR, to Western Europe. This left the Germans seriously undermanned; on the flanks of the Sixth Army, they could only field the 29th Panzergrenadier Division and the 48th Panzer to assist the Romanians, not nearly enough to repulse any Soviet assault.

However the Soviets had their own problems in preparation for the start of Uranus. Initially they wanted to strike on the 8 November, but logistical problems forced them to put back the start date 9 days to the 17 November. The main problems were that the effectiveness of the plan relied heavily on surprise to prevent the Germans from rushing reinforcements into the area. Therefore they had to conceal their build up with logistical problems delaying some units arriving at the jumping off points. The buildups continued, but so did the delays, therefore the Russians decided to postpone once more, for a final time for two days. Operation Uranus therefore was scheduled to start on the 19 November 1942.

By this time the situation in Stalingrad was critical, and this hastened the necessity for a counter-offensive. With Chuikov and the Red Army with their backs to the river in the remains of the city, the Germans became aware of probable Soviet build ups on the eastern bank of the Volga. Through interrogation of captured Russian prisoners of war, the Nazis gained credible indications of Soviet activity and the possibility of an impending Red Army offensive. Despite this, the German high command remained steadfast in the goal to capture Stalingrad and finish off the Russian resistance there. Paulus even asked Hitler if he could withdraw from Stalingrad as a precaution. Hitler refused, choosing to believe instead and incorrectly, that the Soviets had no strategic reserves left; German intelligence seemed to confirm this which only reaffirmed his decision. As early as September, General Franz Halder saw the real danger of the logistics keeping such a stretched front going and warned about the weakening of the flanks of the Sixth Army and 4th Panzer. For his efforts he was dismissed from his post.

On the Russian side, with the Soviet high command, the *Stavka*, there were no such problems of skepticism, defeatism and faulty intelligence that plagued the Germans. They were all too aware of the strategic situation in and around Stalingrad and the logistical issues of their enemy. They had been overseeing the continuation of the buildup for the past two months, and appointed General Aleksandr Vasilevsky to oversee the long awaited relieving of Stalingrad itself once Uranus was underway.

The Soviet 1942 winter offensives comprised of three assaults: Operations codenamed Uranus, Saturn and Mars. Operation Saturn was meant to be continuation of Uranus against the German forces in the wider Caucasus region. Operation Mars (also known as the Second Rzhev-Sychevka Offensive) was to be a separate attack further north against Army Group Centre in the Rzhev district of Moscow. Its purpose was to distract more refreshed forces there and prevent them from deploying south to reinforce the Axis. Operation Uranus involved the large scale use of armour, infantry and mechanized units where the plan was to position on wide fronts where the Axis were too stretched to hold the line to the front and rear of the Sixth Army just to the north and south of Stalingrad. This would prevent the Germans from quickly reinforcing those areas in front of the Red Army. The Russians planned to cross the Volga and commit themselves to a double encirclement of both the city and the open countryside beyond, cutting deep into the rear of the Germans with heavier mechanized units just to the west of Stalingrad. Closer to the city, the Soviets would engage the rear units of the Sixth Army, trapping the Nazis there.

The German high command though was still complacent, they believed that

Stalingrad would yet fall and that the Soviets, was incapable of launching an attack in the south as they were aware of a Russian buildup against Army Group Centre, (Operation Mars). Therefore, in ignorance, they, even at this late stage, continued to deny the possibility (thanks to intelligence stating that the Russians had no reserves), of any imminent offensive.

But the red storm was about to break…

17

The Axis Situation *is* Dangerous

The length of the southern front for Case Blue extended for 300 miles in total, with the Stalingrad campaign stretching Axis forces seriously thin. As well as committing themselves 250 miles to fight in Stalingrad, the Sixth Army was also defending a 99 mile sector of the front line. It was hard to defend in depth over these vast distances as part of Army Group B even though it comprised of the Sixth, and Second armies, 4th Panzer, the weakened but still active 48th Panzer and the 3rd and 4th Romanian armies. Army Group B also had the 2nd Hungarian and the 8th Italian armies as well as another weak German infantry division in reserve. The Germans in the region could field 400,000 troops supported by 402 flightworthy aircraft, the

Italians 200,000 men, the Hungarians another 200,000 and the Romanian armies slightly stronger at 143,296 personnel, 134 tanks and 827 artillery guns. It sounded like a strong force, but the distances covered in the drive eastwards meant that all units were forced to spread out to cover all areas.

The best of the German forces, Friedrich Paulus' Sixth Army and Hermann Hoth's 4th Panzer naturally being busy engaging in Stalingrad meant that the flanks *had* to be covered by the Axis partners, as the Germans themselves usually occupied the centre, spearheading the advance across both Army Groups A and B.

Even with this forced strategic situation, the effectiveness of non-German Axis forces to protect the German flanks didn't bother Hitler, he actually felt quite confident about their abilities in the battlefield. But this trust was rather misplaced; in truth the Axis partners were very much behind in quality, most of their artillery was horse drawn and the rest of their equipment was not much better, it was obsolete. To compound matters, low morale permeated through the Axis ranks due to the unequal and condescending attitude toward the men by the officer classes. Even though the Romanians were only second after the Germans in terms of strength, the mechanization of units left something to be desired. The 1st Armoured Division used the Panzer 35(t), the tanks built in Czechoslovakia and used by the Wehrmacht from 1938 onwards. By late 1942, the Germans were using the more up to date Panzer III and IV models, making the 35(t) out of date, and relegated to use by the Axis satellite countries. The problem for the 35(t) was that its 1.5 inch gun was totally ineffective against the more sloped armoured Russian T-34 tanks.

The Romanian anti-tank guns were also useless. They employed the 1.5 PaK, which had the same sized gun as the 35(t), no good for stopping Soviet armour. To make matters worse, the Romanians were also short of ammunition, for what little good it did them. However, they were not ignorant of the ineffectiveness of their equipment as they persisted to ask the Germans for better guns. It paid off; the Romanians eventually received upgraded 3 inch PaK anti-tank guns to take on the Soviet tanks. Like the Germans, the rest of the Axis manned vast distances, the Romanian 3rd Army occupied an 87 mile stretch of the front to the east of the Hungarians and Italians who themselves were deployed along the banks of the Don River. In comparison, their counterparts in the Romanian 4th Army covered an even greater distance, 170 miles of the line. It was a precarious situation having so many armies knitted together to hold the front; the quality of equipment left something to be desired. The Romanians had their own problems but the Italians, Germany's 'Pact of Steel' partner fared even worse. Their own weaponry was of low quality and they possessed absolutely no anti-tank guns at all. Artillery and mortars were not up to the job and most of the time their hand grenades failed to detonate once thrown. Smaller arms such as machine guns and rifles had to be heated to work, no good in the conditions of Russian winter temperatures. This means that more often than not they jammed or did not fire during battle. This inadequacy meant that Italian soldiers were held in poor regard by their Axis allies, even though in truth they were every bit as professional as their German partners if it was not for their poor equipment. However it was not just them, but everyone, Romanians and Hungarians were also doubted upon by the German commanders, who questioned their ability to fight effectively.

This arrogance and misplaced trust in the combat hardness of the German forces came from a slightly hypocritical point of view; the truth was that the Germans themselves were in no better shape than their allies. After months of relentless fighting, the Germans were considerably weakened and fatigued as the high command failed to maintain their existing mechanized units with fresh replacements. The Sixth Army had suffered a great deal of casualties during the battle for Stalingrad and was seriously depleted in strength. Sometimes the difference between German Panzer divisions were no better than Romanian equipment as they were stretched across a 62 mile front as was with the case of the 11th Army Corps.

To make matters worse, Berlin was worried about an allied landing occurring in occupied France. In response they wanted to deploy a strategic reserve to counter any allied assault in the west. During a critical phase of Operation Blue back in the summer the German high command made a fateful decision; two elite Waffen SS motorised divisions, the SS Großdeutschland and the SS Leibstandarte, two of the most efficient, murderous and ruthless units in the entire German army were transferred out of the Eastern Front and deployed in Western Europe.

The Red Army on the other hand, were managing to raise new units and putting them together to forge new armies to face the Axis front

18

The Red Army Masses...

For the coming offensive, the Red Army amassed a huge force. In total, the Soviet strength was 1,143,500 men (over one-third of the total strength the Germans used to invade the whole of the USSR in 1941), 894 tanks, 13,451 artillery guns and 1,500 aircraft. Opposite the 3rd Romanian Army, the Russians planned to overwhelm the German northern flank so placed the 5th Tank Army supported by the 65th and 21st armies to break through in the Don region and head south. Against the southern flank of the Germans on the Volga, the Soviet Stalingrad Front consisted of the 51st and 57th armies and the 13th and 4th Mechanized Corps. Their objective was to smash through the Romanian 4th Army and sweep north-west toward the town of Kalach where here they would, if all went according to plan, link up with the 5th Tank Army here. For Operation Uranus, the Soviets had massed 11 armies at their disposal consisting of a mixture of tank brigades and corps.

This massive movement contributed significantly to the delays at the start of the operation due to the deployment of such a huge force. But the delays throughout November 1942 was not spent idle; troops in the front areas of the jumping off points rehearsed their orders by practicing war games, mock manoeuvres to counter any such Axis counter attack. Nothing was left to chance, every eventuality was covered, especially the opportunity to exploit a breakthrough with mechanized forces. Even though the Germans had tentative evidence that something was happening, the Soviets had to keep things strictly low-key. This meant employing '*maskirovka*' or deception techniques by camouflaging forces to disguise the build-up, especially from the air, and reducing the risk of detection by cutting down on radio traffic. Security was tight on both flanks with messages passed from unit, to command and divisional headquarters direct by courier rather than radio message where there was a risk that orders may be intercepted. But the Russians knew that radio silence might arouse the Germans' suspicion; it may very well have done as they were getting limited intelligence that there were Soviet movements in the area, even if their intelligence contradicted this. So the Soviets employed a deception trick by deliberately making out that there were increased troop movement in the Moscow area, making the Germans think that any forthcoming Russian offensive would occur further north. Indeed the Russians actually set up dummy fortifications and undertook attacks against Army Group Centre to give the Germans a false impression and make them believe that the Red Army winter offensive would occur in the centre of the Soviet Union. This made the Germans trust their intelligence reports that the Russians had no strategic reserves left. The deception plan went further, anything to make the Axis think the opposite to what was really going on; fortifications were built to make the enemy think that the interrogation reports from captured prisoners were that the Soviets in the south were merely going on the *defensive* only. Fake bridges were built to divert attention from the real crossing points being erected across the Don River in preparation for Soviet units to cross as they attacked. Even with the massive mobilization, Soviet troop movements in the Stalingrad region were still attacked by the Luftwaffe, harassing attempts to deploy. In preparation for the start, engineer battalions were charged with ensuring that the main units and their supplies could cross the Volga safely, but was also ordered to undertake reconnaissance of local Axis movements. These were carried out in the planned breakthrough areas to the south of the city were the Russians were to focus their attacks. Into these regions the Soviets funnelled across the Volga 111,000 troops, 420 tanks and 556 artillery pieces ready to strike. By the 17 November, just 48 hours before the start, events on the Russian side took a political turn. The man tasked with the Soviet counter offensive, General Vasilevsky was summoned to Moscow for a meeting with Stalin. Once he arrived, the Soviet leader produced a letter to Vasilevsky from one of the military leaders, General Volsky who was the commander of one of the participating units, the 4th Mechanized Corps. In it he expressed doubt that Operation Uranus could succeed, citing the condition of the Red Army forces deployed for the upcoming offensive. With so much at stake, doubts were taken extremely seriously; Volsky argued that many Soviet troops had not been issued with adequate winter clothing and as such the offensive was doomed to fail due to the state of the army. Vasilevsky therefore suggested the offensive was postponed to allow for reorganisation or even redesigning it completely. He had a valid point; indeed many Red Army soldiers did lack winter garments and had died of frostbite because the commander's attitude allowed it to happen.

The Soviet senior commanders however overruled Vasilevsky believing Uranus could and should go ahead. Soviet intelligence did as much as they could to gather the fullest picture on the condition of the Axis forces around Stalingrad, but information was unclear on the state of the Sixth Army inside the city itself. In light of this Stalin himself contacted Volsky, who in obedience, some might argue fear, and towing the party line, reaffirmed his intention to carry out the offensive if he was ordered.

Therefore the way to proceed was clear. Operation, Uranus the Soviet Union's main counter-offensive to turn and surround the Germans at Stalingrad was to go ahead. The Red Army had massed, now it was time to strike.

19

The Red Army Strikes

Shortly after 5 a.m. on the 19 November 1942, the Soviets were poised to go in. The attack had been postponed for 48 hours through delays because Zhukov was made aware that the aerial units were not quite ready to go. But now they were all set. At a building in Golubinsky, the headquarters of the Sixth Army, a duty officer received a telephone call; the caller was a German attaché to the Romanian 4th Army Corps in the Kletskaya sector called Lieutenant Gerhard Stöck. He informed the headquarters that he was aware of an imminent Soviet assault within the next few hours. This report was like no other, there were numerous reports of movements across the different front line sectors that turned out to be false alarms, why should this be any different? It was too early in the morning and the duty officer negligently thought it was not worth bothering General Arthur Schmidt, the Army Chief of Staff. It was to be a grave mistake.

On the Russian side, the troops were getting a final dose of patriotic realism, in a final attempt to galvanise the soldiers before the assault. Like a medieval king Stalin addressing his army, sent his men one strong message,

"Dear generals and soldiers, I address you my brothers. Today you start an offensive and your actions decide the fate of the country-whether it remains an independent country or perishes." Such words were grand, but did nothing about the weather. Soviet commanders did consider postponing the initial bombardment due to thick fog which reduced visibility. However the Red Army gunners had spent weeks of preparation and felt confident of being capable to lay down accurate fire. Headquarters decided to proceed.

At 07:20 a.m. the code word 'SIREN' was sent to the soviet artillery positions. Suddenly 3,500 Russian artillery guns opened up, aimed at the Axis units protecting the German northern flank. For the next 80 minutes, the Soviets bombarded the main Romanian 3rd Army blasting everything in their path. The training paid off, shells fell on the soldiers with devastating results all along the front lines; Romanian communications were smashed, forward observation points obliterated and ammunition and supply stockpiles were destroyed in explosion after thunderous explosion.

Many soldiers deployed in the front line areas were killed instantly by the deluge of shells; those Romanians who survived had no choice but to flee for their lives to the rear areas. However even this was not enough as Soviet artillery gunners also targeted Romanian artillery batteries and reserve units further back. Many fleeing troops were also caught out here as well as the Russians targeted these.

But the Soviets were only just getting started.

20

Romanian Targets in the North

At 08:50 a.m. just 90 minutes after the first Soviet guns opened up, the main Russian assault began against the 3rd Romanian Army guarding the German northern flank. The 5th Tank Army supported by the 21st and 65th armies were thrown against the stunned defenders. Despite the bombardment, the first two Soviet assaults were beaten back, but this was largely due to the fact that the Russian fire had churned up the ground, it made it difficult for the tanks to navigate through the Axis minefields safely. This may have been enough to stall the Red Army advance, but the inferior equipment the Romanians suffered compared to their German allies proved decisive. Their lack of adequate anti-tank weaponry, sufficient to penetrate the armour of the T-34 and KV-1 tanks the Soviets used meant that they could not maintain a standard of defence, and so it eventually and inevitably collapsed.

The 3rd Guards Cavalry Corps accompanied by the 4th Tank Corps forced a breakthrough in the Axis lines within hours as the 5th Tank Army also broke through the Romanian 2nd Corps. This was followed by the 8th Cavalry despite the thick fog persisting as they overrun the Romanian and German artillery positions in the rear of the line. This caused utter panic in the Axis order of battle in the field as three Romanian infantry divisions retreated in disarray in the face of the Russian assault. The direction of the offensive outflanked the 3rd Romanian Army on sides, left and right; they were being comprehensively routed.

News from the front lines to the north caused confusion at Sixth Army headquarters. In the chaos, the Germans failed to deploy two armoured divisions, 16th and 24th Panzer to turn and head north to boost the flagging Romanian defence. In confusion, a poor tactical decision was made by the Germans, instead of sending two armoured divisions; they deployed just one weakened and poorly equipped unit, the 48th

Panzer Corps to face the Russian onslaught. It would have been an unequal struggle; the unit could only count on less than 100 tanks to stop the Soviet armour, nowhere nearly enough strength. Commanders had to organise crews into infantry companies because the one vital lifeblood of the machines, fuel was in desperately short supply. As 48th Panzer combatted the Russians they were mauled in the momentum of the assault; the 22nd Panzer Division, attached to the 48th, engaged the Russians with less than 30 tanks. They were almost wiped out in the fighting.

The Soviets began to advance southwards though the weather had started to close in. By now a blizzard began to affect the forces, equipment started to freeze, gun sights became blocked and Soviet tanks began to lose some of their traction as the ground began to become slushy under the mass of laying compacted snow. Despite the weather worsening for the Soviets, it also hampered the Germans, for them the coordination of the Axis response was severely set back due to the conditions in the combat areas.

The 3rd Romanian Army covering the northern flank sectors began to be overrun.

The 1st Armoured Division which was attached to 48th Panzer lost all communication with the Germans. With no direct orders coming through from divisional headquarters they came up against the Soviet 26th Tank Corps. Meanwhile elsewhere, the problems mounting against 3rd Romanian increased. The Russians in their advance and with the Axis retreating, inevitably, the Soviets began to take prisoners. The Soviet 5th Tank Army supported by the 21st Army captured as many as 27,000 Romanians, a sizable force making up almost three whole divisions. Driving southwards, Russian cavalry with their high degree of mobility, pushed through any gaps in the lines, severing communications between the Romanians and the Italian 8th Army to the west. These types of manoeuvre also prevented any possible Axis counter attack once the Soviet advance got so far that their flanks were in danger of being exposed.

The Russians also could rely on almost total air superiority in the sector. So far the Red Air Force had been beaten back time and again, but here the support was much stronger and effective for Operation Uranus. Russian planes strafed retreating Romanian soldiers as they fled from the frontal areas with only the Luftwaffe providing almost nothing in way of opposition, a legacy of the re-deploying of aerial units to North Africa and across occupied Europe. By now the whole northern flank was in utter chaos; the German 376th Infantry Division's flank was initially protected by the 1st Romanian Cavalry Corps, however they failed to prevent the Russians from bypassing the German defence lines. It was not until late in the day on the 19th that the bulk of the German forces began to react to the Soviet thrusts, even though the Romanian 1st Armoured Division was still fighting the Soviet 26th Tank Corps. It was not until the 20th November that they would eventually succumb to tenacious Russian fighting.

But the next day the next phase of Operation Uranus was to begin. The northern flank had been smashed, now the Red Army were about to hit the south.

21

The German Southern Flank

Early hours on the 20th November 1942; the Soviet commander of the Stalingrad Front, Andrei Yeremenko replied to a query by the high command in Moscow, the Stavka. Confirming he would begin his phase of the operation at 08:00 hours that morning as scheduled, he stated he would attack as soon as the fog which had shrouded the area had lifted sufficiently enough. However the weather did not improve by the intended start time, so the decision was taken to postpone the barrage by two hours. Notification of the change was sent out but the 51st Army began firing anyway as originally ordered because they could not be contacted to be informed of the delay. By 10:00 am, the new time of the assault, the Russians opened up on the southern flank of the Germans, manned by the Romanian 4th Army. The 51st Army themselves eventually joined in by attacking the Romanian 6th Corps; the Soviets had the impetus and overran the enemy, taking a sizable amount of prisoners along the way. At the same time the Soviet 57th Army went in, clearing more enemy positions and paving the way for the armoured units of the Stalingrad Front to move forward.

The Romanians stood no chance against the strength of the Russian assault; all the Germans could do was watch as their Axis allies failed to resist for the most part the advances of the Red Army, and were almost wiped out. But the Soviets were not without their own problems; some of their own units failed to decisively exploit the breakthroughs in the Romanian lines meaning they could not push forward with as much haste as they would have liked in the opening battles of the offensive.

By now the Germans had to respond, despite the bulk of their forces fighting within Stalingrad. The only unit free was a reserve outfit, the 29th Panzergrenadier Division which had enjoyed a few small victories against the Russians in the past. It was sent to the southern flank to reinforce the disintegrating Romanian defences in the area. In a bid to stem the Russian tide, it counter attacked the Red Army with successful results. The 29th managed to take out 50 Soviet tanks on the Russian left flank, causing some concern in the Red Army command. However, whereas tactically the 29th had success, overall strategically, there was forlorn hope; the repositioning of the 29th Division removed any effective reserve. Now there was only the Romanian 6th Cavalry Regiment between the Soviets and the Don River.

The Russians had managed to break through on both the northern and southern flanks of the German army. The Romanians had been badly mauled, their lack of decent equipment leaving them totally at the mercy of both the Red Army and the Red Air Force.

And now the Soviets were on the march.

22

Russian Jaws: The Closing of the Trap

On the 20 November, just as the Stalingrad Front was assaulting the Romanian 4th Army to the south, the German 11th Corps was being attacked by the Soviet 65th Army just to the north of the city. This meant applying pressure to the northern end of the Sixth Army in Stalingrad itself. The Russian 4th Tank Corps pressed forward beyond the Germans, but the 11th Corps was not to escape. As the Soviet armour bypassed them, they were attacked from the rear by the Russian 3rd Guards Cavalry Corps. In response, 14th Panzer Division counter-assaulted a regiment of the 3rd Guards Cavalry, destroying it on the flanks. But this engagement was not to prove fruitful; its anti-tank artillery was eventually overrun by the Soviet forces who inflicted heavy casualties upon them. As well as 14th Panzer, the Germans also deployed an additional infantry division, the 276th and a further Austrian infantry unit, the 44th to counter the Red Army drive, but positioning them was delayed at this crucial time as they suffered from a lack of fuel.

By the end of the 20th, the Russians had the upper hand. Making good ground, the Germans were in total retreat from the front as 48th Panzer pulled back, pursued by the advancing Soviet 1st Tank Corps. The surprise and coordination involved in making Operation Uranus work was beginning to show as not only had the Soviets broke through and overwhelmed the Axis forces, they managed to turn the German response. Their advances were rewarded well; by the end of the day, Perelozovsky, a small town 81 miles to the northwest of Stalingrad had been liberated by the Russian 26th Tank Corps.

By the next day, the 21st November, Romanian units in the northern flank were being systematically destroyed in isolation battles. Surrounded and cut off, they were doomed. Meanwhile the Stalingrad Front in the south had punched up to 31 miles behind enemy lines putting the Red Army in a position now to assault the flanks of Paulus' Sixth Army and Hoth's 4th Panzer itself. The Germans tried desperately to hold off the Russians using a small counter attack by 22nd Panzer; but the Soviet armour mauled it, reducing it significantly in strength and forcing it to withdraw southwest away from the fighting.

On the north flank, most of the Romanian 1st Armoured Division was wiped out as the Soviets continued to drive further southeast. The advance was spearheaded by the 26th Tank Corps who adopted a more Germanic style Blitzkrieg strategy by pushing forward relentlessly, bypassing the enemy without getting caught up in rear guard action.

By now panic began to set in as the implications of the Soviet offensive was starting to become clear. On the 21st November, General Paulus received information that the Russians were only 25 miles from the Sixth Army headquarters and if that was not enough, there were no more reserves left to engage the Red Army advance. Meanwhile in the south, the 4th Mechanised Corps continued to push north after a brief pause. The Germans tried to put up a delaying action using garrisons stationed in various towns, but it was not enough to hold up the thrust as they succumbed to superior Soviet forces.

By now the German forces in Stalingrad and the surrounding district were put at risk of encirclement such was the precarious position the Axis forces found themselves in. Hitler, aware of the Soviet push ordered his forces to establish a defensive stance to hold off the Russians; basically telling those to hold fast whatever the cost. In typical Nazi propaganda style to fool the masses, he designated the forces positioned between the Don and Volga rivers as the pompously named *"Festung Stalingrad"* (Fortress Stalingrad). By declaring this, Hitler was explicitly refusing the Sixth Army and the surrounding forces to pull back to safety which would have been the sensible thing to do. But such was Hitler's fascination with Stalingrad, the men in the locality were being ordered to stand and die in the face of Russian opposition; and it was an order that would play straight into Soviet hands.

The Sixth Army, most of the 4th Panzer Army and other units were in a salient that was being pinched north and south by the Russian armies. But poor coordination between Soviet armour and infantry failed to capitalise the fracturing German southern flank allowing the 16th Panzergrenadier to escape the encirclement, and on a wider scale, enabled much of the Romanian 4th Army to escape total annihilation.

By the 22nd November the Russians in the north crossed the Don River and advanced south. Their objective was the small town of Kalach situated 45 miles west of Stalingrad. The town was the scene of an earlier armoured clash between the German Sixth Army and the Soviet 1st and 64th Tank armies back in July and August during Operation Heron, part of Operation Blue during the drive to the Volga. But by now it was not of strategic importance to the Germans beyond being a supply route and thus the garrison located there consisted of nothing more than auxiliary personnel in supply and maintenance matters. Here news of the Soviet offensive did not reach them until the day before and as communications were sketchy, the men in Kalach had no idea what the Red Army strength actually was.

However to the Russians, Kalach was of

vital importance; the main bridge in the centre was a target for capture to disrupt German supply lines. Early morning on the 22nd the Soviet 26th Tank Corps penetrated the town from the north and approached the bridge using two captured German tanks and a reconnaissance vehicle. Firing on the defenders, they completely caught them by surprise. A Few hours later the main Soviet force broke through to the town, completely driving the Germans out as they had no means to adequately defend against the Russian tanks. This enabled another Red Army unit, the 4th Tank Corps to link up with the Russians approaching from the south thus completing the encirclement. By now the trap was beginning to close on the Germans as pockets of Romanian resistance, which had long since disintegrated, could only delay the inevitable.

As the Soviet armies linked up at Kalach, the encirclement of Stalingrad was completed on the 22nd November 1942. Operation Uranus had gone according to plan and in just a matter of days, created a pocket in the Stalingrad region. In this pocket the Soviets managed to trap 300,000 individuals in an area that was no bigger than 25 miles north to south and 31 miles east to west. Trapped in it were Paulus and the majority of his German Sixth Army, part of 4th Panzer (a single corps), a Croatian infantry regiment and two surviving Romanian divisions. Caught along with the men were 100 tanks, 2000 artillery guns and as many as 10,000 trucks. It was a spectacular catch for the Russians but for the Germans the Stalingrad pocket became known as the *Kessel*, (the Cauldron).

By the 23rd November the situation had become stark to the Axis. It was nothing short of a disaster as the fighting continued when the Germans tried to launch localised counter attacks against the Soviet armies to try and break through the encirclement. But it was no good; the Russians were too strong as troops trapped inside the Stalingrad pocket fled east to avoid encounters with Red Army T-34's. The threat of the Russians breaking through the Cauldron and cutting them off from Stalingrad caused chaos in the Axis ranks. This prompted them to quickly retreat toward Stalingrad, abandoning much of their equipment in the process of haste causing roads leading to the city to be turned into dumping grounds, littered with destroyed heavy pieces such as artillery and trucks. Small arms like rifles and helmets scattered everywhere like an indication to the utter panic in the German and Axis forces as they tried to get away. Bridges spanning the now iced over and frozen Don River became logjammed with vehicles as the escape reduced the Axis forces to a rabble in the cold weather. Such was the panic, regard for a comrades life was reduced to nothing, it was like a survival of the fittest; many wounded soldiers who could not move as fast were simply trampled upon by both men and vehicles if they fell. Others drowned in the freezing waters of the river if they attempted to cross the ice on foot and was unfortunate enough to fall through. In other places, Axis troops who were also now desperately hungry turned into savages, scouring and looting Russian villages in an almost inhuman search for any scraps of food they could find. To think the once mighty German Army, reduced to this; it could not have been more different from when Barbarossa was launched just 17 months earlier.

In the middle of all this chaos, the Sixth Army tried for their part to construct some kind of defensive lines even though they were severely hampered by the lack of supplies such as rations fuel and perhaps most importantly, ammunition to fight off the Soviet advance. The weather did not help either, by now the harsh Russian winter had set in. The Germans knew from bitter experience the previous year that the elements could be as cruel as ever to any side exposed in the plummeting temperatures.

What made matters worse for Paulus was that the Romanian defence had now collapsed so any gaps had to be plugged by his own army but it was not possible as the situation deteriorated further. Some elements of the Sixth Army could not hold the line and started to retreat toward the northern end of Stalingrad itself, burning and destroying everything that was not needed for an attempted breakout of the pocket. It was a mistake, in doing so the Germans abandoned their protection from Mother Nature, the winter bunkers and pulled back in the open. This was made a reality when the 94th Infantry Division was caught out and ultimately destroyed by the Soviet 62nd Army. There were very few survivors.

By the 24th November the final few

elements of the retreating Germans finally crossed the Don River. As soon as they were across they finally blew up the bridges to prevent the soviet armour from getting across, but at the same time it sealed the Sixth Army and 4th Panzer inside Stalingrad. This meant that the Germans and others were now completely cut off from the rest of the front line along an encirclement running 200 miles all round; the pocket known as the *Kessel* was now truly complete.

In response to the encirclement, the Russians sensibly decided to strengthen the forces deployed around the pocket. Units of the Red Army intended to assault the Germans to both the south and east of Stalingrad in an effort to reduce the size of the *Kessel* and split the German forces defending it into small groups. Even though the front line facing the trapped defenders inside the pocket ran for 200 miles, the thickness of the Russian trap was only 9.9 miles deep. For now the Red Army could hold out against any mounted German counter offensive, prompting the Soviet High Command to begin planning for the next phase of the operation which was codenamed Saturn.

Operation Saturn was designed to attack and destroy the Italian 8th Army and pushing westwards cutting off all the German forces in the Caucuses. Saturn was set for a start date of 10 December 1942.

Meanwhile even with just the encirclement the Germans were forced to reorganise their divisions. Army group A was reformed into the newly formed Army Group Don which included both the Sixth Army and 4th Panzer trapped in Stalingrad as well as the remains of both 3rd and 4th Romanian armies. The general situation looked increasingly negative for the Germans the initial momentum of Operation Uranus had in fact ground to a halt. A period of calm had suddenly settled on the battlefield as both sides looked to regroup and reorganise.

Both sides were pondering their next moves, but inside the *Kessel*, the outlook for Paulus and the Sixth Army was dire.

But it was about to get even worse.

23

Awful Reality – The Fate of the Sixth Army

By now just 265,000 German and Axis forces, accompanied by as many as 40,000 volunteer Soviets who fought alongside the Nazis were now left in the pocket. They had no choice any more, fighting alongside the 'fascists' was considered high treason which only carried one penalty, death by execution. In total the Germans had 20 divisions each with around 9000 men and 100 smaller battalions trapped by the Russians but such was the direction of their advance, 10,000 Soviet civilians along with another 7000 Soviet prisoners of war the Germans had captured were also caught up in the *Kessel*.

But on a positive note for the Axis, 50,000 infantry troops of the 298th and 62nd

Divisions belonging to the Sixth Army that were deployed between the Romanians and Italians were not captured by the Soviet advances, being pushed to the west, and relative safety. Upon the circulation of the Stalingrad region, the Soviets formed two front lines in the newly captured areas, one facing outward to combat any potential Axis offensive, the other facing inward toward the city and the trapped Germans.

The German senior commanders knew this; on the 24 November, Hitler was advised to not order Paulus and the Sixth Army to attempt a breakout from the *Kessel* by Field Marshall Erich von Manstein despite army chiefs pressing for a breakout to a new line just to the west of the Don River. General Kurt Zeitzler was one such chief; he tried to persuade Hitler to allow the Sixth Army to break out to the west and restore the broken front line at the Don bend. For his part Hitler flew into a tantrum and promptly overruled Zeitzler ordering Paulus and the Sixth Army to stay put. Therefore many army commanders urged Zeitzler to disobey this order and authorise the breakout anyway, but even with his rank, General Zeitzler did no such thing. Field Marshall Manstein himself felt confident that the Panzers could break through the Russian lines and open a corridor to the beleaguered forces. At his Bavarian retreat, in Berchtesgaden, at the Obersalzberg, Hitler asked the head of the Luftwaffe, Reichsmarschall Hermann Goering if the air force could supply the Sixth Army from the air. Goering stated that this could be done with what he described as an "air bridge." After all, the Luftwaffe had done a similar thing to a trapped German corps further north earlier in 1942 when the Soviets launched the Demynask Offensive Operation on the 9 February which caught the Germans surrounded around the town of Demyansk to the north west of Moscow. Lasting until the 21 April, the Demyansk Pocket showed that trapped troops could be successfully supplied from the air alone, prompting Goering (albeit on the personal advice of the Luftwaffe Chief of General Staff, *Generaloberst* Hans Jeschonnek), to make a similar bold statement regarding the Sixth Army. However the scale of the operation varied massively; an entire army had never been supplied on such a scale in such a way before. Allowing the Germans to fight on while a relief force was assembled was what von Manstein thought was feasible for a breakthrough. If the Luftwaffe could do its job, then the ground forces could reach Paulus and his men.

With the assurances from both the army and air force that it could be done, Field Marshall von Manstein was tasked with coordinating and rescuing the Sixth Army in Stalingrad. The codename for the rescue effort was *Unternehmen Wintergewitter*, (Operation Winter Storm.)

The plan did not sit well with all ranks of the German military. It was not popular with Luftflotte 4, the air wing that had been assaulting Stalingrad for months; its chief, Wolfram von Richthofen tried to get the decision reversed. His argument was that the scale was too large, yes the Luftwaffe did supply the Demyansk Pocket, but in Stalingrad the situation was very different. For a start the trapped men of the Sixth Army were far larger in numbers and therefore would be harder to re-supply, not helped by the additional elements of 4th Panzer enclosed as well.

It was a daunting task what was asked of the Luftwaffe crews. It was calculated that the Sixth Army would require an absolute minimum of 300 tonnes of supplies per day, but ideally 750 tonnes just to keep going. However logistically there were problems with this requirement; in the Stalingrad Pocket the Germans only held one airfield at Pitomnik and based on the number of aircraft available they were only able to fly in just 107 tonnes per day. The air drop was to be carried out mainly by Junkers Ju52 transports, specifically designed for this type of role. But there was a shortage of this type of aircraft, meaning that the Luftwaffe had to resort to reassigning part of its bomber force to supply duties. The faster and perfectly adequate Heinkel He 111 bombers were found perfect as additional aircraft.

By the 27 November, Richthofen told von Manstein that there too few planes available to supply the 300 tonnes required by the Germans in the *Kessel*. Based on this information, the seasoned military tactician realised that logistically this was the exact opposite to Demyansk. He compiled a detailed report outlining the virtual impossibility of permanently supplying an army from the air and therefore proposed that only a small linkup to Paulus could be used to evacuate the Sixth Army out of Stalingrad.

Furthermore he made the very tactical argument that even though this would mean that Stalingrad would be lost for the time being, the preservation in strength of the Sixth Army would be retained, allowing the Germans to regain the initiative in due course. It was a very sound idea, but Manstein did not take into account the limited mobility of the trapped Germans and their lack of supplies to assault the surrounding Red Army. Hitler, intent on holding Stalingrad, rebutted his Field Marshall and reiterated that Paulus and the Sixth Army would stay inside the city and Goering's 'air bridge' would be sufficient to supply the troops on the ground until a new offensive would smash the Soviet encirclement.

As the Luftwaffe went ahead with the air supply, their targets were well short of the requirements. Now they were only able to deliver on average a mere 85 tonnes per day in an almost round the clock timetable. It was not uncommon for air crews to fly over 100 missions per day into the Stalingrad Pocket which gave the operation a fast pace. Sometimes more vital supplies were given a low priority due to mix ups in coordination.

This meant that instead of receiving badly needed vital supplies such as medicine and ammunition, troops sometimes got Vodka, black pepper and summer uniforms. One cargo drop even contained a supply of contraceptives.

In the mistaken belief that the Sixth Army was to attempt a breakout of the Soviet encirclement in the early stages, some supply shipments were prioritised deliberately. Fuel was often delivered for the armour divisions over ammunition and even food rations for the men. However the priority was changed when Hitler ordered to hold the city while forces broke in. Even though supplies were being hastily delivered, the transports also evacuated certain personnel out of the pocket. These included technical specialists but mainly the wounded or sick were flown out. Anything up to 42,000 people was evacuated, but such was the desperation of the men to get out of the *Kessel*, the scramble to get on board the planes as they departed was animal like. Some even resorted to desperate measures such as hanging on to the wings of aircraft as they took off down the runways; plunging hundreds of feet to their deaths if they lost their grip as the planes gained altitude in the freezing outside air temperatures.

Throughout December the supply flights continued. The Germans began loading their cargo from an airfield 198 miles east of Stalingrad at Tatsinskaya. This was the main base for the Ju52 transports whereas the He 111's were based nearby at Morozovskaya.

The Luftwaffe was trying its best under orders and with whatever supplies it could deliver to keep the troops trapped inside the Stalingrad Pocket alive. But now the ground offensive to finally, and hopefully relive Paulus and the Sixth Army was about to get underway.

PART III – CATASTROPHE!!

"Fascist Germany is passing through a profound crisis. She is facing disaster."
 (Stalin, 1943)

24

Operation Winter Storm

Operation Winter Storm, the German offensive to break through the Russian encirclement of the Stalingrad region occurred in direct response to the astounding success of Operation Uranus and complete failure and weakness of the German flanks held by the Axis satellite partners. Once the Soviets had closed the trap, the Axis set about reorganising their defences in the area. Those Germans and other personnel trapped in the *Kessel* fell under the overall control of the newly formed Army Group Don, and therefore under the overall command of Field Marshall Erich von Manstein who had been transferred from Leningrad at Army Group North to the south.

The Soviets however started to realign their forces, and tighten the grip on the reducing Stalingrad Pocket in preparation for the next phase of the winter offensive, the launch of Operation Saturn – the drive west toward the Black Sea and the trapping all the Germans in the Caucuses. To the north of Stalingrad was the Don Front, to the south, the Stalingrad Front. Meanwhile the aerial supply by the Luftwaffe into the pocket was continuing, but events were beginning to turn against them. Manstein started to realise that the only way was a successful breakout attempt to relieve the Sixth Army would have to be launched sooner rather than later. The Russians had consolidated their own forces and managed to assemble several armies between the *Kessel* and the new front line in preparation just to the west in a new assault on the German forces around the Chir River.

The Germans were hesitant in assembling their forces; all too aware of the situation on other areas of the front, no fewer than four Panzer divisions were allocated to the push, the 6th and 23rd Panzer of Army Group Don along with the 4th Rumanian Army, and the 11th and 22nd Panzer of the Army Detachment Hollidt which lay just to the north. Accompanying these were three more infantry divisions added to by three Luftwaffe Field Divisions in support for Winter Storm. The problem for the Germans with compiling such as hasty force was getting allocated troops to the front. Transportation conditions were not easy and as such many troops never arrived because either they could not physically get to the start points or in some cases, the commands of many units earmarked for deployment under Army Group Don held back their transfer altogether. Another issue was the quality of the forces involved; the Luftwaffe divisions for example were made up of a mixture of ill-trained army personnel, staff officers and conscripted soldiers; but they were equipped with artillery and anti-aircraft guns. Other units in Army Group Don were severely depleted due to heavy losses sustained after weeks of fighting. Moreover, new and fresher outfits that were promised to bolster the exhausted units failed to arrive on time; again a symptom of the transportation conditions getting reinforcements to the front.

One of the few positive pieces of news from the calamitous assembling for Winter Storm was that at least one of the Panzer divisions, the 11th was at full strength. In fact it was one of the most complete units of the whole of the German army on the Eastern Front due to it being pulled from the army reserve; encouraging for the situation in the south. Another division, 6th Panzer was also relatively fresh being transferred from France, putting the total German strength for the assault at 112,000 men and 650 tanks ready to move on Stalingrad.

Both these decent strength units could have made a significant contribution to Winter Storm, if it wasn't for the Soviets launching a pre-emptive strike against the Germans in the area of the Chir River, a tributary of the Don. This tied down Wehrmacht forces in the Army Detachment Hollidt front north of Army Group Don forcing them to defend their positions.

This prompted Manstein to focus his assault solely on the elements of Hoth's 4th Panzer, those that had escaped the encirclement. Under overall control of 4th Panzer were the 17th, brought in from Orel, 6th and 23rd Panzer, along with the Rumanian 4th Army and the 68th (Known as XLVIII) Panzer Corps as the spearhead for the operation.

Meanwhile, Army Group A in the Caucuses released, rather frustratingly, one of its units, the 57th Panzer Corps to Army Group Don to attach itself to 17th Panzer which was also deployed back to its original area. The 17th did not manage to join the army group's line until ten days later which was a significant delay, exacerbated by the fact that the Soviets were beginning to concentrate mechanized forces in the Chir River area. Manstein had no choice, time was now definitely running out; 4th Panzer would launch Operation Winter Storm as soon as possible.

Even though he was going to punch through the Russian lines with much less strength as he originally hoped for, due in part to the distraction of the Soviet Chir River Offensive, part of his main hope was that Paulus and the Sixth Army would still have enough strength to mount an offensive on the Russian lines facing them, forging a link to Manstein upon the signal codenamed 'DONNERSCHLAG' meaning 'Thunderclap'. The plan of attack was that from the front line, straddling the town of Kotelnikovo, 57th Panzer along with the

Rumanian 4th Army would push forward either side of the rail lines, driving north eastwards toward the Mishkova River. Once here 48th Panzer from the Don would then link up with the main force and when sufficient gains had been made, Paulus and the Sixth Army would then attempt a breakout west to reach von Manstein.

It was a big risk, not only militarily as a potential assault and breakout by Paulus would be costly in terms of both men and equipment, (the supplies the Germans were getting in the pocket were barely sufficient to attempt a move), but also politically. The strategy of the operation would contravene Hitler's express orders of no retreat from Stalingrad whatsoever. However, Manstein hoped that the Fuhrer would see the bigger picture here, and that this is the only realistic way for Paulus and his army to escape the Stalingrad Pocket. Of course Paulus himself would also have to agree to take such a risk as well. Everything was ready. On the 10 December 1942, Manstein contacted Paulus to inform him that the commencement of the relief operation would begin imminently and Operation *Wintergewitter* (Winter Storm) was about to begin.

25

The Soviet Defence

The Soviet defence in the wake of Operation Uranus was tough thanks to the superior strength. An initial force deployed by Marshal Georgy Zhukov consisted of 11 armies but in just three weeks an additional 420 tanks, 111,000 troops and 556 artillery pieces were shipped across the Volga.

Both wings of the Soviet military, the air force and the army had enough resources to yield massive amounts of manpower on the battlefield. Since the encirclements had trapped Paulus, over one million Red Army personnel were involved as the Russians continued to execute secondary operations in the area. Initially the Soviets thought they could destroy the Sixth Army in the Stalingrad Pocket swiftly, and then transfer the bulk of its forces westward to face the Don Front. 890 Soviet tanks organised into 14 separate brigades were also laid between the Don Front and the *Kessel* with 127 artillery regiments, and 13,500 guns in total for support.

In the Russian encirclement, the Soviet 51st Army was deployed on the outermost front facing von Manstein away from the inner front line facing Paulus as the Red Army tried to strengthen their forces there. It had 34,000 troops within its ranks but only 77 tanks, whereas just to the south, the 28th Army had even less armour; just 40 tanks to defend the front. However this number was mediated slightly by the 28th's artillery strength of 707 guns and greater numbers in infantry, 44,000 soldiers in all. On the 9 December, the Russians became aware of a build up by the German 48th Corps in the Don region. In response the Red Army compiled 71,000 men, 252 tanks and 804 guns of the 5th Shock Army to counter any threat from the area.

The fronts created by the Uranus encirclements were not ever meant to be permanent. By now the Soviets were massing for the next stage, the commencement of Operation Saturn, a continuation of Operation Uranus using the former assault's momentum. Intended to drive west and completely cut off all the Axis forces further south in the oil rich regions of the Caucuses; destroying Army Group A in the process. Meanwhile they wanted to crush Paulus first, Stalin personally ordered General Vasilievsky to eliminate the pocket and destroy the sixth Army:

TO MIKHAILOV (PERSONAL ONLY)

1. CARRY OUT OPERATION KOLTSO [RING] IN TWO STAGES.

2. FIRST STAGE : ENTRY INTO BASAROINO AND VOROPONOVO AREAS AND LIQUIDATION OF ENEMY'S WESTERN AND SOUTHERN GROUPS.

3. SECOND STAGE : GENERAL ASSAULT WITH ALL ARMIES OF BOTH FRONTS TO LIQUIDATE GREAT BULK OF ENEMY FORCES WEST AND NORTHWEST OF STALINGRAD.

4. LAUNCH FIRST STAGE OF OPERATION NOT LATER THAN DATE

FIXED DURING TELEPHONE CONVERSATION BETWEEN VASILIEV AND MIKHAILOV.

5. FINISH FIRST STAGE OF OPERATION NOT LATER THAN DECEMBER 23RD.

VASILIEV

With these orders, the Russians hoped to strike while the Germans were still in chaos over the situation in Stalingrad.

But the Germans were the ones to strike first.

26

Von Manstein to the Rescue

The 57th Panzer Corps of Hermann Hoth's 4th Panzer began the drive north eastward on the 12 December 1942, heralding the start of Operation Winter Storm. Starting off from the small town of Kotelnikovo 120 miles southeast of Stalingrad, the Russians had increased the distance between the pocket and the front line. The rescue effort to relive Paulus and the trapped Sixth Army in Stalingrad had begun. At first the German armoured columns made decent progress even though the weather was filthy, rain, and snow fell upon the ground; the 23rd and 6th Panzer pushed through the front line and began to threat the Soviet 51st Army from the rear. Even though a battalion of heavy Tiger I tanks had been due to be the vanguard of the assault, delays meant that they did not arrive at the Don Front for another nine days. But this did not impede progress as the speed of the offensive was quite swift in the face of Russian resistance

The element of surprise worked in the Germans favour. The Soviet high command, the Stavka, did not expect that their enemy would be in a position to launch an offensive so quickly after they were cut off from Stalingrad. During the rapid advance, 6th Panzer moved to overrun the Soviet artillery and had actually managed to capture them intact, causing a measure of confusion with the Red Army commanders. General Vasilevsky wanted to use the 2nd Guards Army to block the advances but was unable to detach it as both 6th and 23rd Panzer continued to overrun the Red Army infantry, which noticeably decreased Russian resistance. Thanks to the Panzer columns moving into rear areas, part of the 51st Army, the 302nd Rifle Division had been smashed by the Wehrmacht and by the end of the 12th the Germans had progressed 31 miles into Soviet held territory.

The Russian reply to such a coordinated attack was to garrison villages in the path of the impending assault. Elsewhere the Soviets failed to put up any sort of decent resistance where their cavalry units were reaching exhaustion after weeks of relentless fighting. It was starting to look grim for the Red Army. However, despite the successes that the Germans enjoyed in the early stages of Winter Storm, reports started coming in that the Russians were applying pressure to 23rd Panzer while 57th Panzer were failing to achieve the same results as other armour spearheads. The 57th had made gains against the Soviets, but were unable to just consolidate their progress within the first 24 hours of the operation.

The next day, the 13 December, 6th Panzer, who had made good progress against the 51st Army, began to engage stiffer Soviet resistance who were making attacks against German positions on the Chir River in the form of the Soviet 5th Tank Army. The Germans managed to cross the first natural obstacle, the Alksay River, moved into a town called Verkhne-Kumskiy and defeated Soviet armour in the process. But the Russians consolidated their positions just to the north around the area of the town setting up an armoured clash between the two.

In the ensuing battle, the Soviets took

considerable losses, but eventually the German tanks were pushed back to the Alksay River but managed to hold onto the town. Such were the losses sustained by the Russian armour it was 6th Panzer who came out of the battle with more tanks available even though they had lost some ground, and for the next three days, fighting between 6th Panzer and the 5th Tank Army raged. The Russians attempted a counter attack both against Verkhne-Kumskiy itself and the German positions on the river but this proved fateful; German gunners managed to pin the Soviets in the town, targeting them with artillery and anti-tank equipment. The Russians stood no chance and was destroyed as the Luftwaffe joined in the assault in support of 6th Panzer.

After securing this success, the Germans broke through once more all across the front line, pressing on further north toward another river, the Myshkova. Despite the fighting in the Alksay River district, 6th Panzer had taken heavy losses in its drive forward causing them to pause briefly to reorganise their battalions and repair any damage to their vehicles. Most of this damage the Russians inflicted on the Panzers at Verkhne-

Kumskiy was rather superficial and was able to be repaired in the field; most tanks therefore were repaired by their crews and brought back to fighting condition, bringing the unit back up to strength once more.

27

The Soviet Response

As the four pronged offensive of 4th Panzer moved forward and Operation Winter Storm fully go underway, the Soviet high command, the Stavka, were forced to re-think their preparations for the forthcoming offensive to trap and clear out all the Germans in the Caucuses in the planned Operation Saturn. By the 13 December, both the high command and Stalin himself agreed to re-deploy the 2nd Guards Army. Authorising their transfer, it was moved from the Don Front, south to the Stalingrad Front.

By doing this, the army with its strength of 90,000 troops would be in a better position to assault the Germans by the 15th as it was organised into three rifle corps, the 1st, 2nd and 13th.

Because of the surprise German offensive

which did actually catch the Russians off guard meant that Operation Saturn had to be altered to account for the new threat. Therefore the Soviets decided to limit the assault to attacking and overrunning the Italian 8th Army which would then, hopefully, allow the Red Army to engage the German front line at Army Group Don in the rear areas, causing havoc and confusion.

This inevitably meant that the general direction of the attack had to change; the Soviets were to drive southeast instead of south meaning that to prepare adequately the start date for the push had to be put back to the 16 December 1942.

But the Russians still had to engage the German forces moving northeast. The 13th Tank Corps aided by the 4th Mechanized counterattacked the advancing Panzers close to the Alksay River. The purpose was not to stop or even turn the enemy but as a delaying tactic while the Red Army could bring up the 2nd Guards Army under command of General Rodion Malinovsky to engage the Germans directly.

Inflicting heavy damage on the German armour columns, as they forced their way further north toward the Myshkova River, better news had come from further south. By now Hoth's drive had begun to stall on the 15th but 24 hours later, the 16 December, the Soviets had begun to launch the counter offensive, Operation Little Saturn by using the 6th Army and the 1st and 3rd Armies in support. It was enough to make the Manstein rethink if or not to continue the offensive as by now the German left flank was under threat from the new Soviet assault as 17th Panzer who had been delayed, finally joined in the fight. Overnight the weather deteriorated through snow and then rain by day; it was not ideal for tanks to advance. Despite this, Hoth resumed his drive north on the 17 December using 6th Panzer in the middle, flanked by 23rd Panzer on the right and 17th Panzer on the left. By the next day, the Germans had driven 40 miles since the start of the offensive but still had another 35 miles to go to reach the *Kessel* and things were to get worse; casualties were beginning to mount for the Germans in the freezing weather as the Russians put up more and more tenacious resistance.

By the 18 December the Germans reached the Myshkova River, forging a bridgehead on the northern bank. In response, the Soviets boosted the powerful 2nd Army that faced the Panzers with the 87th Division, the 4th Mechanized Corps and elements of cavalry corps. That same day, Manstein pleaded with Hitler to allow Paulus and the Sixth Army to attempt a breakout form the Stalingrad Pocket, but as usual, he stubbornly refused.

By the evening of the 19th, 6th Panzer crossed the Myshkova River, but the 57th Panzer failed to make any serious advance against stiff Soviet resistance. To compound matters, reports were coming in from Tatsinskaya that the Russians had reached and attacked the airfield used to fly in supplies. If true, this could spell a serious problem for Paulus and the trapped Sixth Army and forced Manstein to issue orders that 48th Panzer turn and go on the offensive in preference to directing it toward Stalingrad and the *Kessel*.

28

German Inadequacy and Collapse

The same day that 6th Panzer crossed the Myshkova River, General Friedrich Paulus received a visitor, flown in specially. The visitor was an officer from Manstein's intelligence staff, sent to brief him on the strategic position and the general situation concerning the front line of Army Group Don. The description that the officer, Major Eismann gave to Paulus did not go down well with the Sixth Army commander. But Paulus was a tactician; he realised that the best option to try and gather his forces for the secondary phase of the rescue attempt, Operation Thunderclap which was a breakout for the advancing Panzer columns of Operation Winter Storm. This meant that both Paulus and von Manstein were of one mind in relation to the best way to make the attempt work, but had to be commenced as early as possible. However, the plan did not sit well with all members of the Sixth Army, particularly Paulus's senior officers. Some personnel believed that given the overall situation of their own forces against the Russians, the air support the Luftwaffe was giving should be more efficiently coordinated leading to better supplies. This would be the preferable option since given the logistical condition of the German armies; a breakout would not be possible at this time. One such officer who held such views was Paulus' own Chief of Staff, Major General Arthur Schmidt. Paulus came to realise that his officer was indeed correct about the reality of the situation. Given the lack of adequate supplies, months of fighting and lack of fuel, the Sixth Army was in no condition to go on the offensive against the Soviet positions. Plus, Paulus knew that Hitler had stressed that no breakout should be attempted under any circumstances. He was not going to risk disobeying superior orders.

Further to the southeast, Operation Winter Storm was stalling. Even though the 57th Panzer was failing to make any decent progress, they did manage to push the

Russians and breakthrough to the Alksay River and press on. By now forward elements of the relief force were just 30 miles away from the southern end of the Stalingrad Pocket and Paulus. However the Sixth Army lacked sufficient strength to engage the Soviets; it had only 70 tanks and precious little supplies. By now freezing blizzards had begun to cover the entire region seriously impeding the exhausted infantry's ability to fight. Paulus and his men were in no condition to smash out of the *Kessel* and drive south to link up with Hoth.

By the 20 December, German infantry under Hoth's command were nearing total exhaustion from lack of sleep. Despite this they did manage to gain a few more miles forward but by now the Germans were starting to pick up radio traffic. It seemed to confirm the deployment of a new Soviet 2nd Army consisting of three corps massing northwest of Stalingrad. This was an error, the army was there, but it was not northeast of Stalingrad, it was southwest of it, and directly in front of Hoth's Panzers. Soviet strength to face the advance continued to build into the next day; but still the Germans pressed on. By the 22 December, Hoth was only 25 miles from the Sixth Army; Paulus might have a chance to risk breaking out even with his depleted forces if Hoth could get another 10 miles or so. But by now the Russians had hardened; the 5th Shock Army accompanied by the 7th Tank Corps and the 6th Mechanized Corps faced the German tanks. Hoth could not move any further, but the threat to him was too great, he could not stay here on the defensive either.

With fierce Soviet resistance grinding down the German advance, and the Russian winter playing, not for the first time in the east a big part, on the 23 December 1942, Manstein made a fateful decision. The Red Army was still pressing their earlier offensive in the Chir River region; there was no other way, they could not go on, if Paulus could not meet them. Forced with the reality of the situation Manstein discontinued the advance and redeployed 6th Panzer to the southern end of the Chir River defences.

By the 24 December, Christmas Eve, despite the worsening situation in the east, the Germans carried on the propaganda to the public by transmitting a special 'live' programme direct from the fighting,

"Come in Stalingrad."

"This is Stalingrad. The front on the Volga." Came the reply. However what was not revealed was that this message was actually a fake. Live broadcasts from Stalingrad had ceased a week before; the propaganda was designed to convince the public that the fight was going better than the reality of the situation. The truth about Operation Winter Storm was less optimistic and very different to the lies put out on the home front. 4th Panzer were in full retreat along the advance front, as the Russians launched an offensive to drive them back using the 51st Army, 5th Shock Army and the 2nd Guards Army. Hastily making their way back to the front lines of Army Group Don, the starting positions for Winter Storm, the Germans were forced southwards. Because Paulus refused to risk his men breaking out of the Stalingrad Pocket as well as his own forces to punch through, Manstein and the elements of Hoth's 4th Panzer retreated southwards over the next 24 hours. By the 25 December 1942, the Red Army took the town of Kotelnikovo, Hoth's point of departure.

With the taking of this town, the Russians had pushed the German and Axis forces back to the front line where Army Group Don retook a defensive stance once more effectively ending the rescue mission. Operation Winter Storm, the attempt to reach the beleaguered troops inside the Stalingrad Pocket had comprehensively failed. And with it went the hope that Paulus could be rescued. To make matters worse, the Soviets now tried to inflict psychological warfare on their enemy with a special Christmas radio announcement,

"Every seven seconds a German soldier dies in Russia. Stalingrad is a mass grave."

It was accompanied by ticking. Both the sound and the message were continuously repeated all day.

The men of the Sixth Army were now on their own.

29

The Legacy of a Failed Plan

By now the Soviet high command was in a good position, they had taken the initiative on the battlefield and were pinning the German and Axis forces back. Now Operation Winter Storm, the rescue effort had also been defeated leaving Paulus and the Sixth Army trapped in and around Stalingrad at the mercy of the surrounding Russians. Their primary objective was now the overall destruction of all Axis forces in the pocket while at the same time launching a new objective westward to further trap all the Germans in the caucuses in the Red Army winter offensive.

For the next phase the Soviets brought up 630 tanks and 150,000 troops to bear down on 4th Panzer who was by now in full retreat and taking on a defensive stance. Building on the momentum of halting the Axis advance, the 51st Army struck at the Germans between the Aksai and Myskova Rivers with the 7th Tank Corps and 2st Guards Rifle in support.

Over the next three days, movements were rapid on both sides as the fluid situation continued to develop. The flank of 57th Panzer was seriously threatened as the Soviets smashed through the Romanians putting them in a position to mount a southern assault on 4th Panzer in the process. In response the Germans had absolutely no choice but to retreat to the southwest in most areas except in the region of the Chir River. Here 11th Panzer and the 68th Panzer Corps tried desperately to hold on to its defensive positions in the face of the Russian assault.

It worked; 68th Panzer was able to hold of the Soviet attacks beating them back. However reports were coming in that the Russians were hammering the weaker Italian 8th Army with such force that they were close to total collapse. This meant that they were very close to a breakthrough, which could threaten the area behind the German front lines. Further to the west lay the captured Black Sea port of Rostov. The Red Army continued to press the Germans and finally broke through at the Chir River as they pressed on chasing the retreating 4th Panzer back toward the Aksai River in the Rostov Oblast.

In the south, the Russians were starting to break through the Axis front. In the north, the operation to concentrate and reduce the Sixth Army around Stalingrad became a prime focus. As the rapid situation developed in the south due to intense and mobile fighting, the Germans forces in Stalingrad were contained in a stranglehold, a noose that was about to get tighter. It was not long before the men of the Sixth Army were starting to run low on supplies; in some areas they had actually run out completely. It was not long before the Germans resorted to killing their horses and eating the meat just to stay alive. On the 26 December 1942, the soldier Wilhelm Hoffman spoke about the men's predicament,

"December 26. We've eaten all the horses. I'd even eat cat: cat meat can be tasty. The squaddies look like corpses or zombies, searching for anything to eat. They don't even duck from the Russian shells-they haven't the strength to run or hide."

New Year was approaching, but the reality was anything but cheerful for the men trapped in the *Kessel*. The distance between the Sixth Army and Army Group Don was 40 miles; they knew how weak their forces really were even if the commanders on the outside did not; optimism was virtually non-existent.

There was now a very real possibility that the Sixth Army could be wiped out entirely due to Hitler's orders to stay in Stalingrad despite the Russian intention in the south to cut off all German forces in the Caucuses from the middle of January 1943 onwards. The only point of note in credit to Paulus' men in the minds of the German command was that due to the numbers trapped in the Stalingrad Pocket, Red Army operations along other sectors of the front was disrupted as the Sixth Army forced the Soviets to divert useful resources to surround them there. But even though the Germans were tied up around Stalingrad and in retreat in the south, it was those in the south that were to be stunned by the impending Soviet winter offensive, Operation Little Saturn.

30

Red Storm Turns the Tide: Operation Little Saturn

Operation Little Saturn was actually a revised version of a grander Soviet plan to drive the German and Axis forces completely out of southern Russia. Originally codenamed Operation Saturn, it was meant to be a continuation of the earlier Operation Uranus which so effectively surrounded and cut off all the Germans around Stalingrad and away from the rest of the Axis front line.

The Russians hoped to push the Germans back toward not just only the northern Caucuses, trapping all the Axis forces advancing on the oilfields, but also slightly further north toward the Donbas, otherwise known as the Donets Basin in southern Ukraine. This ideally, the Soviet high command hoped, would cut off all the Germans in the south.

With the success of Uranus which trapped up to 300,000 solders around Stalingrad along with parts of 4th Panzer, the Russians wanted to capitalise on the Germans forced on the back foot. The highly ambitious nature of the Soviet offensive codenamed 'Saturn' would eventually be reduced in scale by Stalin due to the Axis offensive Winter Storm and the losses incurred by the armies engaging the Germans and their allies.

With the German lines severely overstretched across vast regions of Russian steppe, Operation Little Saturn aimed not only to drive the German out of the Caucuses but also to apply pressure in the eastern part of Ukraine around Kharkov (Kharkiv), and Izyum; as well as further north in Russia itself around Belgorod and Kursk.

Little Saturn was planned to go ahead on the 16 December 1942, while Manstein was trying to relieve Paulus by pushing north during Operation Winter Storm. The initial aim was to assault and overrun the Italian 8th Army and threaten the German flank. If they could do this, the Soviets could then exploit the breakthrough pressing far behind the enemy lines under the military doctrine of deep battle.

But events had to move fast as the Germans were pushing north toward the Stalingrad Pocket. Therefore the Soviet order of battle at the point Operation Little Saturn commenced was that the northernmost tip was manned by the old Bryansk Front, now known as the Voronezh Front under the command of Lieutenant General Filipp Golikov. To the south of him lay the Southwest Front under General Nikolai Fyodorovich Vatutin and below him was Konstantin Rokossovsky's Don Front. Facing Paulus himself, completing the line on the southernmost flank was the Stalingrad Front (later renamed the South Front) under the command of Andrey Yeremenko.

31

First Phase – December 1942

The first part of the winter offensive came about to counter the threat from Operation Winter Storm from its initial attempt to finish off Army Group A in the Caucuses. On the 16 December 1942 the Soviets launched Operation Little Saturn just as General Rodion Malinovsky started to block Hoth's Panzer drive north with his 2nd Guards Army between the Alksay and Myshkova rivers. Strategically, the whole plan rested on cutting off the German and Axis forces moving north to rescue Paulus via a massive westward moving pincer just to the south aimed toward Rostov.

The initial action saw the General Vatutin's Southwest Front move in from the north to attack the Italian 8th Army with the 1st Guards Army commanded by General Fyodor Kuznetsov alongside General Dimitri

Lelvushenko and his 3rd Guards Army. The surprise and ferocity of the assault by the two Soviet armies completely overwhelmed the Italians because Lelvushenko committed both the 17th and 25th Tank Corps to his attack to accelerate the breakthrough before advancing toward the town of Millerovo close to the Ukrainian border.

On the 17 December the 25th Tank Corps went in at 11:30am penetrating, along with the 17th Tank Corps deep enough into enemy territory with the aim of pocketing and cutting off the Italians from the Germans. The Russians succeeding in encircling 130,000 of them along the Don River and were now in a position to threaten Army Detachment Hollidt in the west. Further on from this, the 25th Tank Corps then moved on to Morozovkaya just to the east of the Luftwaffe base at Tatsinskaya.

Unlike the Romanians, the Italians put up a slightly stronger resistance against the Russians. Fierce fighting raged between the two sides as the Red Army inflicted increasing numbers of casualties upon the Italian troops, outnumbering them 9 to 1 as they fought each other for almost two weeks.

After nearly 14 days of fighting though, the 8th Army could not hold out for much longer forcing Manstein to divert 6th Panzer to aid their Axis ally. Over the next 24 hours the fighting was murderous and savage, especially on the trapped Italians; out of the 130,000 that was encircled, 85,000 were killed, leaving just 45,000 who survived to meet up with the Germans.

Further south, the 1st Panzer Army was threatened with their own encirclement by the Soviet 28th Army as they pushed forward with the 51st Army in support assaulting the Hoth's German relief column. The whole purpose of these two advances in accordance with the Soviet deep battle doctrine was to try and cut off the forces of Operation Winter Storm. If that was not bad enough, the Red Army was about to deal a hammer blow. During this phase, the Russians broke through on the 23 December with General Vasily Badanov reaching the town of Skassirskaya with the 24th Tank Corps, attached to the 3rd Guards Army. They advanced on to reach, by early on the 24 December, Tatsinskaya airfield; the base from which the Luftwaffe were flying in desperate supplies to the beleaguered Sixth

Army trapped in the *Kessel.* Goering's 'air bridge' to Paulus was in danger of being wiped out.

Operations were still going on inside the base as no advance warning was given of the imminent Russians attack. The Soviets assaulted the base directly with tanks from three sides as they surprised the Germans by breaking into Tatsinski military airport. The Germans responded well by hitting the Soviet tanks with artillery guns and infantry shooting grenades. Several Russian tanks therefore exploded, killing the occupants inside, but it was not to last. The tenacity of the Soviet assault meant that the Nazi defence was soon overrun as Red Army infantry soon joined the armour in the battle for the airfield. This caused panic amongst the German pilots, and many were mercilessly shot dead as they ran to their planes by Russian soldiers as the tanks continued driving through thick snowstorms as the weather continued to deteriorate. Over the coming hours, Russian armour took advantage of what should have been a vitally important installation for the Germans. With Luftwaffe defences trying to defend the base neutralised, the Soviet tanks roamed the airfield destroying anything that could be of use to the Germans including the precious transport planes, some of which were new and still on their railway cars waiting to be unloaded.

Under heavy fire, the workers were forced to evacuate the airfield as the Luftwaffe personnel frantically tried to get as many aircraft in the air as possible under the Russian attack. By now though, the tanks were beginning to run low on ammunition so resorted to ramming the aircraft with the tanks themselves. In total 300 planes (according to the Soviets) were left burning wrecks, (the Germans said only 72 planes had been lost), as 16 Ju86's and as many as 108 Ju52 transports managed to get into the air, pulling back to Novocherkassk.

The Luftwaffe now had no choice but to establish a new base at Salsk, which only further exacerbated the aerial supply efforts to the Sixth Army. With Tatsinskaya in Soviet hands however, the 24th Tank Corps found itself cut off and low on supplies, with no chance of replenishment.

General Badanov knew that during the taking of the airfield, his position was isolated when the German forces from the north followed his support, the 24th Motorised Brigade, cutting them off. However by the 26 December, the same unit began engaging the Germans, breaking through to join up with the main body of the Russian advance but by now the Germans forces were reacting. 56th Panzer had been diverted to deal with the deep advances the Soviets had made against both 6th and 11th Panzer who had managed to cut off Badanov's 24th Tank Corps along with the 1st Guards Army as well.

The Germans also started to block the Russian advance further to the north coming up to reinforce Badanov while simultaneously they tried to destroy him in an effort to retake the vitally important airfield. Bringing forward two infantry divisions, the 306th and 579th, the Germans launched the attack accompanied by three armoured trains in support to engage the Russian armour.

The Soviet high command ordered more forces to assist Badanov by pressing the 1st Mechanized Corps and the weakened 25th Tank Corps to reinforce him with just 25 tanks left after heavy fighting. They themselves were reinforced by infantry units but could not break through to the airfield. By the 28 December, Badanov and the rest of the 24th Tank Corps had little choice but to attempt a breakout themselves to get out from the Germans after being given permission by the high command. The Russians knew such a move would be costly, and so it proved as many Soviet personnel were killed and most of the tank corps lost in the breakout fighting. Badanov and his unit had penetrated up to 150 miles from their base, proving that formations could conduct operations deep in the German rear areas. However they did have to rely on captured supplies to keep going.

Despite the Germans successfully engaging Soviet follow up infantry thus cutting off Badanov in the first place, the Tatsinskaya operation proved that the Wehrmacht and the Axis were vulnerable if the Red Army could get behind the front line units. This forced the Germans to rethink some of their strategies, but for the Soviets, the raid provided a lot of valuable experience and a lot to learn. It gave the Russians the encouragement to create new tank armies with greater autonomy from their central command structures and this gave them the ability to maintain operations deep in enemy territory allowing for a higher degree of freedom. But on the flip side, the breakout operation showed that such deep operations and the opportunities the deep battle doctrine could bring would also carry a greater element of risk; and it could be costly in terms of both men and machine.

Even though the Russians suffered devastating losses in the breakout from Tatsinskaya, they had done their duty; due to the destruction of many transport planes, the Luftwaffe operation had been severely set back, many air crews and ground personnel had been killed, forcing them to withdraw. And because the air operations were disrupted, so was the supply line to Paulus and the men of the Sixth Army trapped around Stalingrad.

The raid on Tatsinskaya was a major defeat for the Germans and a major victory for the Soviets. Previous such raids were badly thought out or coordinated, usually carried out by lightly armed cavalry units, a thought regarding mobility rather than potency in battle. Airborne forces had the advantage of being dropped anywhere the plan required but were too lightly equipped and could not do significant damage even when military units were operating alongside partisans and resistance cells. The armoured thrust and raid showed that this type of offensive could work if prepared for properly. And the better prepared, the more devastated the enemy was likely to be.

By the end of the battle, the Soviets claimed to have destroyed 84 German tanks and 106 guns from artillery pieces to anti-aircraft emplacements, many forming the Luftwaffe defence of Tatsinskaya airport. In addition 5000 Axis prisoners fell into Soviet captivity with another 12,000 killed.

Such was the fluid situation, the events at the airfield and the continuing Russian assaults forced Manstein to turn his forces back as Operation Winter Storm began to fail. But on a wider scale, the reduced plan of Operation Little Saturn gave a little bit of breathing room for the German forces of Army Group A who were further away from the Stalingrad area around the oilfields and Caucuses. For fear of being cut off themselves the commander Ewald von Kleist issued the order to evacuate the Caucuses, pulling his forces away to the north and back to the Kuban, the area bordering the Black

Sea and the Sea of Azov around the Kuban River and Taman peninsular. The only exception to the retreat was that of 1st Panzer which was directed to Rostov to join the Don Front. Even though Operation Little Saturn had been reduced down to check the German counter offensive, it had achieved one of its aims, to drive the Axis out of the Caucuses.

But the job had not been done yet. It was a new year, and the next phase was about to begin.

32

Second Phase – January 1943

As 1943 dawned, the pendulum of momentum had most definitely swung away from the Germans and toward the Russians. General Golikov's Voronezh Front attacked with four armies on the 16 January heralding the second phase of
Operation Little Saturn. This new offensive, aimed at the Hungarian 2nd Army which was deployed on the Don River came under furious attack from the Red Army. Soon the Hungarians were surrounded in the area of the town of Svoboda, and at the mercy of the Soviets. They like the Romanian and Italian contingent of Army Group B before them stood virtually no chance; like other Axis partners, they too were destroyed, annihilating them as a credible fighting force on the eastern front.

Meanwhile the troops around Stalingrad were still receiving whatever Luftwaffe supplies they could, even though the

Germans main base at Tatsinskaya was lost. But by the middle of January things were about to take a catastrophic turn; their new base at Salsk was itself now forced to be abandoned by the Soviet advances. The Luftwaffe had no choice if they wanted to stay in operating range of the *Kessel* to keep Paulus and his troops alive, but to move the town of Shakhty. There lay a rough airfield facility nearby at Zverevo, it was not the best, but it would do the job in the most appalling of conditions.

The Soviets, aware that the Germans had moved there, decided on the 18 January to finish off the relief effort for good by wave after wave of attack on the facility. It resulted in the loss of a further 50 Ju52 transports; a heavy blow to the Luftwaffe, but this was only just the tip of a very large iceberg. The weather was now frigid as technical issues grounded some planes, due in part to the cold weather freezing machines. To make matters worse for the Germans, and increase the futility of the relief effort was that any planes that did take off on their desperate journey had to fly over enemy territory to reach the Sixth Army. Along the supply routes the Russians had concentrated anti-aircraft fire. The effect was devastating on the Luftwaffe, moreover the Red Air Force were now back in increasing numbers, intercepting the transports mid-air in attempts to shoot them out of the sky. These compounding matters meant that the Luftwaffe lost in total 488 precious aircraft.

Even with the deteriorating situation, the air supply effort continued with difficulty, and supplies did actually manage to get through. But it was nowhere near enough to keep the soldiers alive never mind munitions to keep fighting. The men of the Sixth Army were by now, slowly starving to death in the freezing cold and beleaguered conditions. Malnutrition was beginning to spread as the men became ever weaker day by day. Such conditions were hard to imagine from outside of the Stalingrad Pocket but anyone who saw the conditions now endured would get a very real and shocking sense of the state of the men. Pilots and air crews of the transports that got through the Soviet barrage were the ones to witness this.

By January, they had begun to notice that once cargo had been delivered, many of the troops were just too tired or weak to unload supplies from the aircraft. Hunger also prevented them from functioning adequately. Conditions like this turned men once more into animals; soldiers on the same side, comrades in arms, friends and blood brothers now turned on each other, fighting for even the smallest scraps of bread. It was an inhuman and shocking sight to witness.

In Berlin, as far away from the chaos at Stalingrad on one could get in terms of both distance and condition, Hitler started to become rather angry. His rage was focussed on one of his commanders, General Kurt Zeitzler, who found out after Martin Bormann told his master that he had been limiting himself to starvation rations in solidarity with the men of the Sixth Army at Stalingrad. Hitler immediately ordered the general to start eating normally once more, (a total disregard for the awful plight of his troops trapped in the pocket). Not wanting to disobey his commander in chief, Zeitzler, who by this time had lost 12 kilograms in weight, did what he was told.

Meanwhile in southern Russia, the situation was dire for the Germans. The Luftwaffe groups were suffering punishing losses, 328 aircraft were damaged to a point they were no longer airworthy with another 160 destroyed outright. The Heinkel He 111 bombers that were allocated to transport duties were hit, 165 destroyed along with Junkers Ju52 transports, at least one third of the fleet were taken out, some 266 planes. In other areas, 9 Focke Wolf Condors, 5 He 177 bombers and 42 Junkers 86's were also lost. But it was not just machines, aircrews, experienced from other theatres of war elsewhere were also killed, almost 1000 in number. These crippling losses had a severe impact in the combat ability of Luftflotte 4; at least four of its units had to be dissolved due to the depletion in both men and planes.

For the Axis, the situation on the ground was just as bad if not worse as that in the air. The Germans were again threatened with yet another encirclement when the 2nd Army was attacked just to the north. However this time they reacted more swiftly and managed to escape the Soviet trap, retreating west toward eastern Ukraine throughout the rest of January.

The Italians though were not so lucky; at this point elements of the 8th Army had up until now been largely unaffected by the battle in the reserve areas due to the Soviet offensive on the right flank further east. The

Italians here consisted of 4 units, the 156th Vicenza Infantry, and 3 additional Alpine (Alpini) divisions: the 2nd Tridentina, the 3rd Julia and the 4th Cuneense. Their good fortune to be out of the way was about to change when the Russians encircled and destroyed the Hungarian 2nd Army at Svoboda once the Red Army launched the next phase of Operation Little Saturn on the 13 January. Once this was achieved the Soviets then assaulted and pushed back the German 24th Army Corps on the left flank of the Italians and the Alpini units. This left them in serious danger as it proved when the Russians attacked them as well.

In response to the Soviet attack, the Alpini divisions fought back, holding the Russians, but the Red Army managed to advance either side of the Alpine divisions covering 120 miles in just three days. This, like the Hungarians and the Sixth Army, trapped the Alpini, forcing them to retreat by trying to break out despite orders to hold the front line at whatever the cost. The Italians did not obey, and by the 15 January, began to prepare to fall back. These preparations took two days under heavy fighting until late on the 17th when they were ready to move under the order of their commanding officer, General Gabriele Nasci, however by this time the Italian Aplini units were taking heavy damage.

The Italian Tridentina Division, (which was the only division still able to fight effectively) and assisted by a few Germen armoured vehicles led the Italians and Alpini joined by other trapped Hungarians and Germans out and to the west; some 40,000 people in two columns all to their destination, the new Axis front line in eastern Ukraine. The Soviets were hampering them from the air, had occupied every village across the area and were hammering the soldiers of the Tridentina, making them fight for every settlement in bitter battles conducted between the Axis and the Red Army. Still the Italians, Germans and Hungarians pushed onwards, covering a distance of 200 kilometres on foot over the course of the next two weeks. In those 14 days, they fought the Soviets in no more than 22 separate battles as they made their way west. Times were hard; fighting and moving by day, the soldiers were sickeningly and cruelly exposed at night in the vast, remote

Russian steppe, enduring freezing winter temperatures that plunged to -40 ℃.

However on the 24 January the badly mauled Cuneenese Division decided to break away from the stragglers and form their own column. They marched southwards alone through the Russian occupied territory fighting through every village to clear a path to the west.

By the 26 January, the remaining rabble of soldiers and the vanguard of the Tridentina reached a small hamlet called Nikolayevka, the last enemy settlement before reaching the Axis front line. Although tiny, the Soviets decided to defend it, occupying the locality with as many as 6000 Red Army troops. 4000 Alpini soldiers who were able to fight took on the Russian defenders trying to clear the block with four battalions, the Vestone, the Verona, the Valchiese and the Tirano. The Soviets held off the Alpine divisions hour after hour, which for retreating Italian troops were pretty effective against the more heavily armed Russians. Time was not on the Axis side as Russian reinforcements could arrive at any time, making their task almost impossible to achieve as both sides fought each other for the advantage.

Vicious fighting raged as the Italians tried to advance; the Alpine Edolo Battalion assaulted the Russians, leading to the killing of Brigadier General Giulio Martinat, the corps Chief of Staff. The breakthrough finally came when this prompted the Tridentina Division Commander. General Luigi Reverberi to order his men forward while riding on one of the remaining usable Panzer tanks left, effectively leading from the front. Inspiring the men, all 4000 Italians advanced with their superior officer toward the Soviet positions, and opened a gap between the Russian lines with the use of the tank. It was enough to persuade the stragglers along with the 5000 Germans and Hungarians alongside them to push forward to desperately smash through the Red Army encirclement line before it could be strengthened.

Numerically inferior, the Soviets tried to fight off the advancing Axis force, but suffered huge losses as many Russians soldiers were killed in the face of such a large wave of troops. Despite bitter fighting, the Axis pressurised the Russians forcing them to fall back and abandon the village. The Red Army no longer assaulted the Alpini retreat, freeing them to move west. But further south it was a different story for the Cuneenese, by the morning of the 28 January they had covered a distance of 200 kilometres by walking and had engaged the Russians a total of 20 times. This took an extreme toll on the division who by now had lost 80% of its men. The frozen sub-zero temperatures and the heavy fighting almost decimated the outfit. Their misery was not to be prolonged; that same day, the last pitiful remnants were slaughtered by Soviet Cossack forces. 4th Cunaneese Division was completely wiped out. Symbolically, the survivors of the 1st Alpine regiment burned the Cuneenese regimental flag declaring the doomed unit extinct as it ceased to exist.

Meanwhile after the events at Nikolayevka, the straggling surviving remnants of the 3rd Julia Corps, (just 4250 soldiers out of 15,000) the Germans and Hungarians, led by just one third Tridentina who had also survived although exhausted, wounded and frostbitten finally reached the Axis front line in the Kharkov region by the 1 February under the stewardship of General Reverberi, who was seen as an Italian national hero.

By 5 February, the Soviets of the General Golikov's Voronezh Front had pushed the Germans back to Kharkov and Kursk, as the Axis tried to set about organising a strong defensive line in eastern Ukraine. However by now, even though the Russians had succeeded in pushing the Germans back across all fronts in the south, and virtually knocked out their Axis allies out of the war, they themselves became stretched. It would eventually set the scene for more bloody battles in the coming 12 months, most notably the Third Battle of Kharkov, and significantly, the organisation of Operation Citadel, the German 1943 summer offensive, which would eventually result in the Battle of Kursk.

But for the moment the Germans had been thrown back. Now the focus would turn to Paulus, the Sixth Army and Stalingrad once again.

33

Operation Koltso – Russian Victory

On the 10 January 1943, just as the Soviets were throwing the Germans and the Axis back and out of southern Russia, the Red Army begun their offensive to deal with the Germans trapped in the *Kessel*. Forming part of the final phase, their aim was the annihilation of the enemy and the long awaited liberation of Stalingrad itself. Codenamed Operation Koltso (Operation Ring), the plan was to shell the Germans, forcing them to retreat into the city, where they would have nowhere to go.

No fewer than seven separate Soviet armies began the offensive on the 10th with a massive artillery barrage, pounding the German troops in their defensive positions before attacking. For the next three days fighting raged between the Sixth Army and the Soviets and by the 13 January the Red Army had taken heavy losses, half the tank force knocked out and 26,000 men killed. Undeterred, the Russians relentlessly pushed on for the next four days, capturing the entire western side of the pocket thus reducing the size of the *Kessel* by half.

Due to the intensive nature of the fighting, the Red Army had become rather disorganised in their push forward so were forced to pause only briefly to regroup. There was no danger of a German counter assault so the Russians repositioned their forces for the next phase which commenced on the 20 January. Reorganised, the Russians made a push for the German held airfield at Gumrak; this was vitally important as it was the last held airfield available for supplied to be flown in. The Germans had to hold on but just two days later, on the 22 January, the Russians took it as they advanced, finally killing off the vital supply line to the troops. That same day General Friedrich Paulus sent a message by radio to his superiors in the German supreme high command, the *Oberkommando des Herres*, or OKH,

"Russians in action in 6 km wide on both sides Voroponovo, some with flags unfurled to the east. No way to close the gap.

Withdrawal to neighboring fronts who are also without ammunition, useless and not feasible. Supply with ammunition from other fronts also no longer possible. Food at an end. More than 12,000 unprovided for wounded in the encirclement.

With this message, Paulus was saying that the Sixth Army no longer the capacity to fight and sustain an effective resistance. He continued,

"What orders shall I give the troops who have no more ammunition and will be further attacked with heavy artillery, tanks and massed infantry? Fastest decision necessary because dissolution in some places already started. Confidence in the leadership still exists."

Here Paulus was giving the high command the full and frank picture of both the supply situation and morale situation in both the command structure and the wider leadership. Although the mention about the dissolution signalled that on the ground, some of the men were already starting to feel abandoned, by Hitler especially. Their scepticism was well founded; with the devastating loss of the airfield, the Sixth Army was condemned; there was now no other facility to land aircraft to deliver supplies, meaning that everything had to be delivered by parachuting it in. In addition to this, because no planes could land, the wounded had absolutely no chance of evacuation, and rescue from the increasingly deteriorating situation.

By now the Sixth Army had no choice but to retreat, there was no way that given the condition they were in, could they sufficiently hold the line in the countryside. Supplies gradually dwindled, then became exhausted as they fell back, diminishing the hardness of Germans resistance to the Soviet advance. Therefore in the light of this, the Germans were forced even more on the defensive and to retreat back into Stalingrad itself. On the 24 January, things were looking incredibly bleak, the reality, and the resignation was beginning to set in with the men as noted by Lieutenant Helmut Quantz in a letter home,

"My dear brother! Sorry about the messy handwriting, my hands are frostbitten and my head's confused. We'll never get out of here. The breakthrough won't happen. We're all dead here it's just that we don't decompose, because of the Russian frost."

Other soldiers began to realise the truth. By now their belief in victory was non-existent, and was completely unwilling to believe in the German leadership no longer. One soldier summed up the truth in a letter,

"I was horrified when I saw the map. We're quite alone, without any help from outside. Hitler has left us in the lurch. Whether this letter gets away depends on whether we still hold the airfield. We are lying in the north of the city. The men in my unit already suspect the truth, but they aren't so exactly informed as I am. No, we are not going to be captured. When Stalingrad falls you will hear and read about it. Then you will know that I shall not return."

Others were now beginning to suffer at the very limit of their physical endurance as another man recalls,

"My hands are done for, and have been ever since the beginning of December. The little finger of my left hand is missing and - what's even worse - the three middle fingers of my right one are frozen. I can only hold my mug with my thumb and little finger. I'm pretty helpless; only when a man has lost any fingers does he see how much he needs then for the smallest jobs. The best thing I can do

with the little finger is to shoot with it. My hands are finished."

By the 25 January, fighting raged inside the city once more as the Russians squeezed the Sixth Army ever tighter. By now dissent was starting to permeate the German ranks as the reality of the futileness of the overall picture began to set in. This was not however realised just quite yet by Paulus who was now holed up in his new inner city headquarters, the Univermag Department Store in the city centre, (after he was forced to abandon his previous headquarters at Golubinsky), decided to quell such attitudes. Relieving command of the 51st Corps from its commander Walther von Seydlitz-Kurzback, he was punished by Paulus because, realising the obvious, left open the possibility of surrendering to the Russians with his divisional commanders. Paulus was not going to let one unit act like that, for the fear of spreading the idea that surrender was the preferred option to fighting. Relieved of his command, Seydlitz later deserted from the German side, surrendering himself to the Soviets in person.

The next day, the 26 January, the Russians advanced through Stalingrad toward the hill

Mamayev Kurgan, the scene of such bloodshed earlier in the battle. The 13th Guards Division linked up with elements of the Soviet 21st Army which proved critical; the enemy, being beaten back in savage urban fighting street by street, block by block, was now pressed into two separate pockets. In the end, the Russian assault had succeeded in cutting the German Sixth Army in two.

The northern pocket, led by General Karl Strecker, the commander of the 11th Corps, was situated in the industrial areas to the north of the city centre, concentrated around the tractor factories. Meanwhile, completely cut off, with the Russians between them was Paulus himself and most of the senior Sixth Army commanders in the southern pocket concentrated around the centre of Stalingrad. It was here that the Red Army focused their assault over the course of the next five days, destroying the coherence of the Germans in bitter street fighting as they were flushed out and slaughtered wherever they could be found. By the 24 January, Paulus received direct orders from Hitler regarding the hopeless situation,

"Surrender is forbidden. 6 Army will hold their positions to the last man and the last round and by their heroic endurance will make an unforgettable contribution towards the establishment of a defensive front and the salvation of the Western world."

With this order, he had hammered the last nail in the coffin of the Sixth Army. By the 31 January, Hitler, backhandedly, promoted Friedrich Paulus to the rank of Field Marshal; knowing that no German Field Marshal had ever been captured, the logic was clear; he expected Paulus to shoot himself. Paulus however, confided in his staff with a rebellious remark,

"I'm a believer, I'm a Christian. I reject suicide."

Meanwhile the same bloody fighting had fractured the Germans as they were pinned down into separate buildings, fighting for their lives in hails of bullets as the southern pocket disintegrated around them. The Soviets fought heavily for, and managed to clear the city centre of Stalingrad as they approached Paulus in the Univermag Department Store. Surrounded on all sides, and virtually out of all ammunition and other supplies, German resistance effectively ceased once the Russians reached Paulus' door.

Entering the headquarters, Russian staff officers attempted a peace negotiation with Paulus, who remained, even when staring defeat in the face, irritatingly stubborn. Instead the Soviets entered into a terms settlement with his colleague General Arthur Schmidt to try and stop the battle. The Russians wanted a German capitulation as soon as possible, but Paulus refused to sign an order for the troops in the southern pocket to surrender and further denied having the authority to order the northern pocket to cease fighting, even though he was still the overall commander of the Sixth Army.

This stubbornness prolonged the battle, and therefore would invariably cause more deaths amongst the soldiers. With the southern pocket shattered in reality, the entire might of the Soviet armies was now bearing down on Strecker's northern pocket around the tractor factory. Despite it being an industrial urban location, albeit ruined after months of heavy fighting, the Soviets poured in intense artillery fire; shell after shell fell upon and around the shattered Germans in an attempt to reduce their resistance. Any remaining bunkers that provided some kind of shelter was then assaulted with tanks, or short range artillery firing directly upon them, killing any occupants inside. Despite this and the mounting German losses, General Strecker still refused to capitulate believing, along with Nazi propaganda that the longer he held out, the more Red Army troops he could tie up and help the general situation in other regions on the eastern front.

By February, the Germans, battered, bruised, wounded, exhausted and starving while enduring -30 ℃ temperatures were now at the very limit of their tolerance. Many soldiers suffered severe frostbite, to the point where their fingers simply snapped off. The Russians by now had smashed the Sixth Army, who was all but finished after being stunned by massive Soviet attacks. By the 2 February in the early morning, one of Strecker's officers had gone over to the Red Army side to negotiate surrender to the Soviet forces. Faced with the reality of the situation, General Strecker finally came to terms and accepted the inevitable in a final radio message back to Germany stating that the army had done their duty to the last man.

With this message resistance by the Sixth Army had effectively ended, and the cost was high. Out of the 210,000 Germans left in the Stalingrad Pocket to face the final assault, 60,000 men were killed, either during the fighting or in the weeks after through suicide. Approximately another 90,000 men surrendered directly into Soviet captivity while 35,000 had been fortunate enough to be evacuated by air. Out of all this, just 10,000 hard core elements remained to fight on fanatically against impossible odds

The Sixth Army capitulated as the battle for Stalingrad was lost. Just over two and a half years earlier, in 1940 when the invasion and occupation of France (and its humiliation was assured) the same men marched through the capital, Paris in a massive victory parade, past the Arc de Triomphe and down the Champs Elysees. It was a typically proud display of German superiority over their enemy in the warm summer sunshine.

But now, in 1942, those same men of a supposed 'master race' were lying dead, on the frozen Russian expanses; many others, shelled and shocked, and themselves humiliated into a pitiful surrender against a race their own indoctrination considered subhuman and inferior to 'pure Aryan blood'. The surviving men of the Sixth Army had indeed been abandoned, and left for dead, either at the mercy of the Soviets, or the brutal Russian winter.

The German Sixth Army had finally been destroyed. After 199 days, the Battle of Stalingrad was over.

34

After the Guns Fall Silent

No amount of propaganda could disguise the disaster on the Volga. Even though events dictated otherwise, no positive news came out of the area even though the German public were officially kept in the dark about the events in Stalingrad and southern Russia until the end of January 1943. By now, just days before the actual surrender of the Sixth Army, they were told the truth even if it was tinted with a typical Nazi slant.

On the 31 January regular programming schedules on the state radio were disrupted all over Germany, replaced by sombre music to ready the public for the news. The music played, taken from the Seventh Symphony's Adagio movement by Anton Bruckner played out across the airwaves before the official German announcement,

"Stalingrad had fallen to the Soviets. The Sixth Army had fought courageously but had succumbed to vastly superior enemy forces and to unfavourable circumstances."

It was a vague and understated announcement. Hitler himself later believed that the two day delay to 4th Panzer around Voronezh back in July was fatal in allowing the Soviets to reinforce defences in Stalingrad itself. Perhaps these were part of the 'unfavourable circumstances' they referred to?

But the Nazi government did acknowledge for the very first time a setback in the war effort publicly, and this was no ordinary defeat given the scale of the disaster. But the catastrophic impact of it was overwhelming, even though the Germans had suffered defeats elsewhere in Russia this was different both psychologically and materially. Up until now, the Soviet Union had endured three times as many losses as the Germans on the battlefield; but now those losses suffered at Stalingrad were virtually equal, something the Soviets could sustain, but Germany could not.

Even though the main Sixth Army had surrendered, the elements that refused to lay down arms fought on in the belief that dying by the bullet was better than the conditions endured in Soviet captivity. Some solders that continued to resist may have been brainwashed to the National Socialist idea and Germany's final victory even if that would mean them losing their lives to achieve that aim. Many used letters to boast to their families back home in Germany that even though they realised the gravity of the situation, and they were not going to escape the *Kessel*, they were proud to *"Sacrifice themselves for the Fuhrer."*

Such a statement as this was clear blind loyalty to a fanatic who did not care about their welfare, guided by an ideology representative of death, suffering and misery. In the ruins of Stalingrad the horrors of the battle were laid bare. Trenches ran across vast areas of ground, and through bombed out buildings. In the bottom of them lay the corpses of dead Germans, frozen green in the cold alongside dead, frozen grey Russian soldiers. Accompanying them were other pieces of blown up human flesh, limbs and extremities. Helmets, different shapes from both sides, littered the ground, now half filled with snow.

Away from the disgusting sights, In Germany, the Nazis used the public mood and the Stalingrad defeat to galvanise the nation to a point where all of its resources, heavy industry and agriculture could be used for the continuing war effort. On the 18 February, at the Sportspalast venue in Berlin, Minister of Propaganda, Joseph Goebbels gave a famous speech, long and rambling urging all Germans to take part in the struggle. He utilises some dubious arguments to reinforce his case; during the speech he attempts to rationalise the events at Stalingrad,

"The tragic battle of Stalingrad is a symbol of heroic, manly resistance to the revolt of the steppes. It has not only a military, but also an intellectual and spiritual significance for the German people. Here for the first time our eyes have been opened to the true nature of the war. We want no more false hopes and illusions. We want bravely to look the facts in the face, however hard and dreadful they may be. The history of our party and our state has proven that a danger recognized is a danger defeated. Our coming hard battles in the East will be under the sign of this heroic resistance. It will require previously

undreamed of efforts by our soldiers and our weapons. A merciless war is raging in the East. The Führer was right when he said that in the end there will not be winners and losers, but the living and the dead."

The German defeat was a stark lesson to the military about the tenacity and tactical awareness of the Soviets on the battlefield. These 'coming hard battles in the East' are a sign that the Nazis were all too aware that the Russians could deploy huge numbers of troops in battle and were willing to sacrifice them if necessary to achieve victory, whatever the cost. As for his remark on 'previously undreamed of efforts by our soldiers and weapons' meant that in reality, Germany could no longer rely on its Axis allies and must carry the burden of battle alone. The truth was that the Wehrmacht and its logistical abilities were in the end, woefully inadequate in the field. He continued on rambling to a delirious and brainwashed crowd, this time talking about the necessity for a total war effort,

"The total war effort has become a matter of the entire German people. No one has any excuse for ignoring its demands. A storm of applause greeted my call on 30 January for

total war. I can therefore assure you that the leadership's measures are in full agreement with the desires of the German people at home and at the front. The people are willing to bear any burden, even the heaviest, to make any sacrifice, if it leads to the great goal of victory."

No they were not, the soldiers were becoming rather despondent especially in Stalingrad that they had been abandoned and left to die and the leadership did not care about their condition in the cold. Many felt that they were not fighting for Hitler, but only for survival, which was true. Only the hard line fanatics carried on the fight ideologically. As for the 'leadership's measures in full agreement with the German people', that was also a lie. The hierarchical pyramid structure of the NSDAP meant that subordinates were always required to obey superiors. This only benefitted Hitler in what was known as the Fuhrer Principle, (*Fuhrerprinzip*). As for the general public, they were 'persuaded' by the propaganda machine orchestrated by Goebbels himself. All who did not go along with the running of the state were watched and punished by the Gestapo, a metaphorical knife to the nation's throat.

Next he tries to attack another of Germany's enemies, England,

"The English maintain that the German people has lost faith in victory.

I ask you: Do you believe with the Führer and us in the final total victory of the German people?

I ask you: Are you resolved to follow the Führer through thick and thin to victory, and are you willing to accept the heaviest personal burdens?

Second, The English say that the German people are tired of fighting.

I ask you: Are you ready to follow the Führer as the phalanx of the homeland, standing behind the fighting army and to wage war with wild determination through all the turns of fate until victory is ours?

Third: The English maintain that the German people have no desire any longer to accept the government's growing demands for war work.

I ask you: Are you and the German people willing to work, if the Führer orders, 10, 12 and if necessary 14 hours a day and to give everything for victory?

Fourth: The English maintain that the

German people is resisting the government's total war measures. It does not want total war, but capitulation!

I ask you: Do you want total war? If necessary, do you want a war more total and radical than anything that we can even imagine today?

Fifth: The English maintain that the German people have lost faith in the Führer.

I ask you: Is your confidence in the Führer greater, more faithful and more unshakable than ever before? Are you absolutely and completely ready to follow him wherever he goes and do all that is necessary to bring the war to a victorious end?"

This was nonsense; no real large scale subversive actions were taken in Germany. Indeed the allies were worried that if Hitler ever died, he may have become shrouded in martyrdom, steeling the Germans to fight on, or even worse, another fanatic may take his place. As for his statement, 'Are you absolutely and completely ready to follow him wherever he goes and do all that is necessary to bring the war to a victorious end?' Calling for legitimised mass murder perhaps? And certainly an argument to say that total war must be implemented to preserve destruction from any of Nazi Germany's enemies. He finishes with a rallying cry,

"When the war began, we turned our eyes to the nation alone. That which serves its struggle for life is good and must be encouraged. What harms its struggle for life is bad and must be eliminated and cut out. With burning hearts and cool heads we will overcome the major problems of this phase of the war. We are on the way to final victory. That victory rests on our faith in the Führer.

This evening I once again remind the whole nation of its duty. The Führer expects us to do that which will throw all we have done in the past into the shadows. We do not want to fail him. As we are proud of him, he should be proud of us.

The great crises and upsets of national life show who the true men and women are. We have no right any longer to speak of the weaker sex, for both sexes are displaying the same determination and spiritual strength.

The nation is ready for anything. The Führer has commanded, and we will follow him. In this hour of national reflection and contemplation, we believe firmly and unshakably in victory. We see it before us, we

need only reach for it. We must resolve to subordinate everything to it. That is the duty of the hour. Let the slogan be: Now, people rise up and let the storm break loose!"

The notion put forward of 'total war' was the call to arms in the wake of the catastrophe in the east to intensify the conduct of the war anywhere, even in the west. Still, even after the disaster, Goebbels was still trying to justify that Hitler was the best person to conduct the army rather than the generals?

Meanwhile in Stalingrad, while Goebbels was ranting and raving in ignorant defiance, those who believed and heeded his ideas continued to resist even though the fighting had stopped. Those who remained, usually SS fanatics and those who refused to believe in defeat, stayed behind in a futile guerrilla warfare campaign hid out in cellars and even the sewers as the Soviets continued their mopping up operations. In one basement, the soviets found 18 SS men who refused to give themselves up; allowing no quarter, the Russians made no hesitation in killing all of them. Not all held out in cramped conditions, others hid more openly in trenches or huts as they were gradually flushed out and liquidated by the Red Army well into February. By the 20th, many pockets of armed resistance had now ended, but some continued on into March 1943 where the last isolated pockets were destroyed where the NKVD reported that the last remaining Germans lost 2,418 killed with a further 8,646 captured and sent to POW camps in the east.

But what about the fate of those Germans who had surrendered legitimately at the end of the battle? Weakened by starvation and disease ridden due to a lack of adequate medical care during the encirclement, the Soviets had no regard for the welfare of an enemy they considered fascists. In huge columns stretching for miles across the Russian landscape, ordinary soldiers and junior officers were sent on the so-called death marches east to both labour and prison camps all across the Soviet Union, notably Siberia. The Russians treated their German captives brutally, mistreating them which resulted in appalling deaths, some from various diseases such as typhus; so much so that as many as 27,000 prisoners died within the first three months with another 35,000 eventually being transported to their final destinations. Not all prisoners were shipped eastwards however, some were kept back in Stalingrad itself to help with the reconstruction of the devastated city (which begun as soon as possible after the battle). For many, it was a survival of the fittest, disregarded by their own leadership, their captors were no better; malnutrition and overwork took their toll as well as the bitter cold as many of the injured suffered fatal infections to the wounds initially sustained in the fighting. As the reconstruction began, army sappers had to clear mines and dud munitions for safety, marking special safe routes for people to work on. 200,000 people worked to rebuild; embarking on the grisly task of burying the dead first. But such was the horror of the battle that not all could be found straight away; bodies were still being discovered even after the war itself. Years later, two of these bodies were discovered, by now skeletal remains, one German, one Russian; both had, in the fury of combat stabbed each other with their bayonets at the same time before mutually being covered by rubble from a nearby shell blast. By the middle of March 1943, the phone lines in the city were once again operable as things were salvaged, including the vital Tractor Factory which was by now once again churning out tanks for the Red Army refitted from damaged vehicles.

If you were fortunate enough to be a senior officer, then your treatment was marginally better due to your rank. Some of the captured Sixth Army senior officers were paraded in Moscow as a prize for the Soviet propaganda. Paulus himself, after being taken to a house just outside Stalingrad after his surrender (and proposing a toast to the Red Army) was exploited in a Soviet attempt to undermine German morale especially in the wake of the defeat by becoming the main signatory (amongst other officers as well) of anti-Hitler statements. Paulus always denied having ever being captured, rather preferring to state that he was surprised by the Red Army; in relation to this he also assured the families of those captured that they were indeed safe, despite the brutal conditions and the fact that many had died already.

Paulus did not see his homeland again until well after the war. He returned to Dresden in what was now the Soviet occupied East Germany, still technically a prisoner, trapped behind the Iron Curtain in the post-war,

Europe in a Cold War world. He always defended his actions at Stalingrad for the rest of his life, but for the surviving men he disastrously led into battle, they were still imprisoned in the east, now just 5000, eventually came home in repatriation to West Germany in 1955, ten whole years after the war itself had ended.

This was the immediate legacy of Stalingrad. Not just the military defeats, but also the human cost to both sides, before, during and after the battle and further, into the post-war world.

35

Casualties

When the Germans surrendered, out of the 90,000 taken prisoner were Romanians of the Colonel Voicu Detachment accompanied by survivors of the 20th Infantry, and 1st Cavalry Divisions, some 3000 people in all. In total, across all theatres of Operation Blue, including the fight for the oilfields, the drive to and the fighting in Stalingrad as well as Soviet Operations Uranus, Little Saturn and Koltso, the Axis losses were high. The Italians suffered 110,000 casualties while the Romanians and Hungarians were all but destroyed. The Romanians had to rebuild after incurring losses of 160,000 troops while the Hungarians could only field an army again in 1944 after it had 143,000 of its men killed or wounded. In all from July 1942 to February 1943, up to 850,000 men on the Axis side were killed, wounded, missing or captured across both the ground and air forces. A great deal of Axis prisoners died within Soviet captivity from illness, wounds, mistreatment and malnutrition. In total between 1943 and their release in 1955, 85,000 prisoners of war died in the Soviet internment camps.

The Russians themselves suffered appalling casualties during the struggle. For a start, 750,000 persons were killed, wounded or captured in Stalingrad itself; further afield across the whole of the southern front the Soviets lost 478,741 men killed or missing in action with a further 650,878 wounded. As a whole, the Soviet Union's losses were 1,129,619 men dead or wounded as a result of the Axis drive into southern Russia.

In addition to the military dead, the civilian dead made for stark reflection. Up to 40,000 Soviet citizens died in Stalingrad when the Luftwaffe bombed it as a prelude to the German invasion by the Sixth Army and 4th Panzer. It is a certainty that many more innocent people were killed in the countryside across the whole of the region. Despite these disturbing figures, the Soviets did not waver from their victory. One Red Army soldier wrote to his wife,

"I'm in an exceptional mood. If you only knew, you'd be just as happy as I am. Imagine it -- the Fritzes are running away from us!"

In all the battle of Stalingrad and the wider operations resulted in the deaths of up to 2 million people on both sides. The sheer scale of the slaughter made Stalingrad different to other battles and a destructive symbol of the ideological harshness of the struggle in the east.

CONCLUSION:

"The god of war has gone over to the other side."
 (Hitler, 1943)

36

One City too Far

The Battle of Stalingrad changed the mood in Germany. It was also one of the great tuning points of the Second World War, the moment when the momentum shifted from Germany and the Axis to its enemies, and not only in Russia. Just after Stalingrad, Hitler commented somewhat philosophically,

"What is life? Life is the nation. The individual must die anyway. Beyond the life of the individual, is the nation."

Part of this momentum came about because of the difference in attitude between both Stalin and Hitler in regard to the freedom both leaders allowed their military staff to influence the conduct of the war.

Before Stalingrad, Stalin himself took on a rather autonomous role in regards to military matters, dictating the deployment and tactics of the Red Army. However, as the battle progressed he allowed his generals, such as

Zhukov and Vatutin amongst others to plan and take the initiative on their own, especially during the counter-offensive battles of Uranus and Little Saturn. The victory at the airfields of Tatsinskaya showed that well organised deep battle doctrines could work and units could work effectively on their own or under regional orders. However the Red Army was not always perfect; drunkenness was rife in the ranks whenever the men could get hold of alcohol, which often lead to fights. Looting was another problem as they passed through liberated villages, taking anything they could, which soured somewhat celebrations from poor villagers who greeted them. This was not entirely surprising as many units were not always stocked with supplies, so livestock made for tempting sources of a good meal. Another aspect of the Red Army in the wake of Stalingrad was that as they advanced, many orphaned young boys were picked up. This was a cruel legacy of the Germans invasion, as many of their parents were either killed in the fighting, or murdered by the SS– the *Einstatzgruppen* as the Wehrmacht passed through. This meant that many children were part of partisan resistance groups in occupied areas and were not adverse to seeing violence. Many of these youngsters were absorbed into army units as mascots and assigned minor duties like watching captured prisoners. On one occasion, one boy was asked by the men of his unit to watch over a caught German solder. Unprompted, the boy without mercy gunned him down. Such orphaned children who had lost their siblings had to be cared for by the Soviet state, what better way to serve the Motherland than to be conscripted into the army? As time went on, these kids were drafted into the line as replacements for losses incurred by front line units, reducing the average age of the Red Army soldier into the teens. Despite these issues in the ranks, the decision for Stalin, who was himself, a dictator like Hitler, put more trust and faith in his army command thus allowing for greater flexibility in the field by experienced commanders. This was in stark contrast to the Germans. Hitler did not fully trust his generals and field marshals, something which increased as the war went on as events started to turn against the Wehrmacht. The *Fuhrerprinzip* (Leader Principle) that was the core of the Nazi internal doctrine gave absolutely no room for negotiation between the military high command and the German leadership. In the early stages of the war when Germany was enjoying stunning successes albeit with a few setbacks, the military had no reason to question Hitler's tactics in conducting battle. As the tide turned however, especially in the late stages of the war, the better judgement and experience was often overruled by Hitler, in part to the Leader Principle, but also driven by a belief that he knew better than his commanders. Indeed, this was fuelled by the fact that in the First World War, Hitler had served in the trenches on the front line; his generals came from aristocratic Prussian stock and therefore were merely cavalry or artillery officer so had no 'real' experience of fighting. As time went on, and as the defeats mounted this inflated egotistical attitude swelled in Hitler's psyche to the point where he would dismiss any logical suggestion like a strategic withdrawal, even to the point where he would fire staff on grounds of defeatism. This effectively halted any such flexibility in the German army on the front lines as generals were forced (for fear of being dismissed from their posts or worse), to make irrational and sometimes suicidal tactical decisions in battle. During Stalingrad, the Chief of Staff, General Kurt

Zeitzler became increasingly confrontational with Hitler, over his refusal to withdraw troops from overextended positions. For his part Zeitzler tried many time to resign, but Hitler curiously never allowed him to; a sign of the *Fuhrerprinzip* having an abnormal grip on not just the NSDAP, but the military as well. German rigidity played directly into the hands of Russian flexibility on the eastern front. Even so, that was no assurance that the Soviets would keep winning every battle; directly after Stalingrad the Soviets tried to launch further offensives, Operation Gallop to advance to the Sea of Azov and Operation Star, to capture Kharkov. This lead to the Third Battle of Kharkov during February and March 1943 where the Germans counter attacked and defeated the overstretched Russians in eastern Ukraine, racing to capture the city and crush the Soviet summer offensive. In July, the Germans, using a combination of Army Groups Centre and South, decided to attack a bulge in the lines centred on the town of Kursk. Codenamed Operation *Zitadelle* (Citadel) it was intended to *"get the Russians back for Stalingrad"* by attacking a huge salient into which the Red Army had well prepared defences. This led to The Battle of Kursk, the largest tank battle ever seen anywhere in the world, initially successful but were eventually turned and defeated, especially in the south in a large engagement fought around a village called Prokhorovka. Both Kursk and Operation Citadel was a failure and indicative of the slow loss of territory the Germans were enduring after the defeat at Stalingrad. These losses, compounded by events on other fronts elsewhere in Europe led to the steady deterioration of the German war effort and the slow decline of the Third Reich. By 1944, with the allies already in Italy and now had just landed at Normandy in France, the Soviets launched Operation Bagration against Army Group Centre. This huge Soviet offensive destroyed the eastern front for the Germans, liberating Smolensk and Vitebsk, pushing on into Belorussia and kicking the Wehrmacht out of Minsk, forcing them west toward Poland. Army Group North was forced back, outflanked and trapped in the Baltic States where it would remain until the end of the war. Army Group South was pushed back through Ukraine as the Red Army strove to drive the Nazis out of the Soviet Union for good. The Russians liberated Warsaw and Poland after a brief but bloody uprising just as the Red Army got to the outskirts of the capital. Staling was perfectly happy to see any Polish nationalist patriots fight against oppression; why risk his own troops when the Germans could do the job for him? By now with the situation dire for the Nazis, the three army groups of the eastern front had been reorganised into Army Groups A & B, but it was a futile effort. Finland had been knocked out of the war, the Soviets were pouring into the Balkans, and to make matters worse, Romania had switched sides, joining the Russians in the fight against Hitler. The Third Reich was fracturing, and now the Red Army was poised to enter Germany itself. By April of 1945 the Soviets had encircled Berlin, Fascist Italy had collapsed, France and the Low Counties had largely been liberated by the allies and western Germany was overrun. The final act came when the Red Army went into the Nazi capital in another urban battle that would prove every bit, if not even more brutal as Stalingrad a mere 26 month earlier. In the midst of total carnage the Germans fought for survival, but it was no use, the war was destined to be lost. Hitler himself was beset with backstabbing and treachery in his most senior and oldest party ranks. Goering, now down in Bavaria telegrammed his master asking if he could take command as Fuhrer according to his 1939 decree. Hitler responded by stripping him of all his offices and ordering his arrest by the SS. Heinrich Himmler, the evil head of the SS and overseer of the horrors of the Holocaust fled and attempted to negotiate a peace settlement with the western allies but not to the USSR (he wanted to keep fighting them) through a Swedish intermediary named Count Folke Bernadotte. When Hitler learnt of this he could not believe it. By the end of the month, everything was lost, the Reich in ruins, ultimate defeat looming and the failure of an SS army under the command of Colonel Steiner to abandon the western front on the Elbe River and relive Berlin. With forces only getting as far as Potsdam, there was only one course of action left. Like a coward and with public support for him virtually collapsed, Adolf Hitler committed suicide deep underground in the *Fuhrerbunker* below the *Vorbunker* underneath the Reich Chancellery around 15:30pm on the 30 April 1945 via a cyanide pill in the mouth and a bullet in the head. Just over one week later, Nazi Germany unconditionally surrendered. The Third Reich collapsed; the Second World War in

Europe was finally over. Stalingrad illustrated two significant things. The first was that it exposed just how weak and ill equipped Germany's Axis partners really were, even though they had fought with some degree of distinction and bravery against overwhelming odds. The Italians, Romanians and Hungarians were too far out of their depth in the frozen and vast expanses of Russia. Secondly the battle launched the Soviet Union as a world power. For the first time, its armed forces managed to take the initiative in battle, outwit and outmaneuver their opponents and carry that on toward final victory. After Stalingrad the Soviet high command, the Stavka, had increased faith in both the commanders but also the units and gave greater autonomy to their operations in successive theatres of conflict. After the war, the Soviets occupied the counties it had overrun, installing puppet states; including East Germany after it was divided up into post-war occupation zones forming a 'buffer zone' and proclaiming them part of a grand alliance termed the Warsaw Pact. The military and industrial might gave the Soviet Union increased respect and influence on the world stage even when the grand alliance between east and west broke down in mutual suspicion dividing the continent with an 'Iron Curtain' and plunging the world into the tenseness of the new Cold War.

But if it was not for Stalingrad, and the sheer stubbornness of the Russians to hold the Germans there, heeding Stalin's orders to take *"Not one step back!"* and therefore preventing their advance any further east, then history may have been very different. Even though the Soviet Union itself eventually collapsed in December 1991, The Battle of Stalingrad would forever be known as one of history's bloodiest fights, but in the interest of both freedom and eventual democracy in a modern post-Cold War, world in both the west *and* the east, it was a sacrifice that was a necessity.